SHADES OF REFLECTION

EXPLORING DUALITIES

PARTH AJIT KHAJGIWALE

Made with ♥ on the Notion Press Platform
www.notionpress.com

To My Parents and My Elder Brother,

You are the unwavering pillars of support on this incredible journey of exploration. Your boundless love, encouragement, and belief in my creative pursuits have fueled my passion for writing and the exploration of dualities. Through the highs and lows, you have stood by me, providing the strength and inspiration to delve deeper into the complexities of life. This book is a tribute to your unwavering faith in me and a reflection of the values and wisdom you've instilled. With heartfelt gratitude, I dedicate these pages to you, for you are the true authors of my story.

With love and appreciation,
Parth Ajit Khajgiwale

Contents

Contents

Contents

Preface

In the complex tapestry of human existence, we often find ourselves entangled in the intricate dance of dualities. These dualities are the threads that weave through the fabric of our lives, shaping our decisions, our beliefs, and our very identities. They are the contrasting forces that challenge our understanding of the world and ourselves.

"*Shades of Reflection: Exploring Dualities*" is an invitation to explore these profound contradictions that define the human experience. This book beckons you to embark on a journey through the landscapes of contrasting aspects and perspectives, where one side may appear virtuous but harbors shadows, while the other may seem flawed but holds noble intentions.

Within these pages, we venture into the depths of our own psyche, contemplating the delicate balance between ambition and obsession, self-confidence and arrogance, freedom and anarchy. We traverse the terrain of society, pondering the fine line between justice and revenge, diversity and division, tradition and stagnation.

Our exploration takes us through the realms of the individual, where we examine the complexities of traits like kindness and naivety, resilience and stubbornness, and humility and self-deprecation. We also traverse the global stage, contemplating the implications of environmentalism versus extremism, diplomacy versus appeasement, and collaboration versus exploitation.

In each chapter, we seek to understand not only the dual nature of these concepts but also the profound impact they have on our lives, our communities, and our world. Through stories, philosophy, psychology, and real-life examples, we delve deep into the rich tapestry of human existence, where contrasting forces shape our thoughts, actions, and choices.

It is important to remember that these dualities are not meant to provide definitive answers but to provoke thought and introspection. As you journey through these pages, you will encounter both the light and the shadows within yourself, and you may find that the line between good and bad is not always clear-cut. Instead, it is often blurred and shifting, as we grapple with the complexities of the human condition.

"Shades of Reflection" is an invitation to embrace the ambiguity, to question the boundaries of morality, and to discover the profound beauty that emerges from the interplay of contrasting forces. It reminds us that our humanity lies in our capacity to reflect, adapt, and grow in the face of these dualities.

As you embark on this exploration of dualities, may you find insight, inspiration, and a deeper understanding of the world within and around you. Join us on this quest to uncover the many shades of reflection that shape our lives and our shared human journey.

Welcome to "*Shades of Reflection: Exploring Dualities.*"

Parth Ajit Khajgiwale

Acknowledgements

This book, "Shades of Reflection: Exploring Dualities," has been a labor of love, exploration, and self-discovery. It is with immense gratitude that I acknowledge the individuals who have contributed to its creation, shaping not only the words on these pages but also my own growth as a writer and thinker.

First and foremost, I extend my heartfelt appreciation to my parents and my elder brother for their unwavering support. Your belief in my creative pursuits has been a constant source of motivation. You are not just my family but the true authors of my story.

I am indebted to my professors, mentors, and fellow students at the International Institute of Information Technology Pune, who have nurtured my passion for both technology and the written word. Your guidance and encouragement have been invaluable.

To my friends and peers who have provided constructive feedback and engaging discussions, I thank you for your candid insights, which have enriched the content of this book.

I also extend my thanks to the countless authors, philosophers, and thinkers whose works have inspired and influenced my writing. Your wisdom continues to shape the thoughts and ideas presented here.

The words of Shah Rukh Khan in Jawan—*"Main kaun hoon, kaun nahi ... pata nahi ... maa ko kia vaada hoon, ya adoora ek iraada hoon ... main acha hoon, bura hoon, punya hoon, ya paap hoon ... yeh khud se poochna ... kyun ki main bhi aap hoon"*—made me realize the duality within a person and how one can achieve self-realization. Shah Rukh Khan has been a true inspiration to me, and this realization has profoundly influenced the essence of this book.

Lastly, to the readers who embark on this journey of exploration with me, thank you for your curiosity and open-mindedness. It is my sincere hope that these pages will provoke thought, inspire reflection, and spark meaningful conversations.

"Shades of Reflection" is not merely a book; it is a collective effort and a celebration of the human capacity to ponder, question, and learn. Each one of you has played a part in its creation, and for that, I am profoundly grateful.

With deep appreciation,

Parth Ajit Khajgiwale

CHAPTER ONE

Desire's Dance: Balancing Ambition and Obsession

In the grand tapestry of human existence, ambition and obsession stand as two compelling, yet divergent, threads, weaving intricate patterns of desire and determination. These twin forces are born of an innate yearning that courses through our very being—a yearning for accomplishment, for recognition, and for the fulfillment of our deepest aspirations. Though they spring from the same well of longing, their journeys diverge significantly, resulting in vastly disparate outcomes that can shape the course of our lives.

Ambition, in its purest form, is akin to a radiant star on the horizon, a luminous guide that beckons us to embark on a journey of self-improvement and achievement. It is a potent elixir that instills in us an unwavering belief in our own potential, encouraging us to scale the summits of our dreams. Ambition inspires us to set audacious goals, to push the boundaries of human capability, and to embrace life's challenges as stepping stones towards personal and societal progress. It is a virtuous companion, urging us not only towards individual success but also towards the greater betterment of our communities and the world at large.

In contrast, obsession emerges as the shadowy twin of ambition, often masquerading as its virtuous counterpart. Obsession is a relentless specter that descends upon the soul, compelling an individual to fixate unyieldingly on a single objective, often to the detriment of all else. While ambition whispers the wisdom of balance and discernment, obsession is a ravenous beast that blinds its victims to the broader canvas of existence. It narrows one's vision to a single, all-consuming point, skewing the perception of success and rendering them incapable of adapting when the tides of circumstance inevitably shift.

The vital divergence between ambition and obsession can be discerned in their approaches and consequences. Ambition is a voyage of self-discovery, rooted in the desire for growth and holistic excellence. It teaches us patience, adaptability, and the wisdom to discern when to advance and when to pause in our pursuit of greatness. Ambition aligns with our core values, fostering a balanced existence that encompasses not only our professional aspirations but also our personal lives, relationships, and well-being. It is a compass that guides us through life's intricate maze, reminding us that success is not merely a destination but a journey where each step holds significance.

In stark contrast, obsession demands unrelenting devotion to a single goal, often heedless of the journey's inherent significance. It is a siren song that leads one astray, driving them relentlessly towards their chosen endpoint, regardless of the toll it exacts. Obsession blinds its devotees to the beauty of the path, causing them to ignore the toll exacted on their health, relationships, and emotional well-being. It is a tunnel-visioned approach that may ultimately culminate in personal burnout, fractured relationships, and the unforeseen consequences of a myopic focus.

In the essence of this profound duality lies a profound lesson about the complexity of human desires. It underscores the fact that the pursuit of greatness is not a linear odyssey but a multifaceted expedition. It is a journey characterized by the nuanced choices we make, a delicate dance between the guiding light of ambition and the perilous depths of obsession. Ultimately, it is these choices that shape the legacy we leave behind—an inheritance of measured ambition that seeks excellence while honoring the intricate tapestry of our lives, or a legacy of unchecked obsession that exacts a great personal and societal toll.

As we delve deeper into this labyrinthine exploration, we encounter the potential for both brilliance and ruin, each choice a fork in the road, each decision a turning point in our narrative. It is in this delicate balance, this interplay of ambition and obsession, that we find the true essence of human existence. We are both the sculptor and the clay, shaping our destiny with the chisel of our desires and the wisdom of our choices.

Consider the painter, tirelessly perfecting each brushstroke, seeking excellence in every hue and shade. This is ambition personified—a quest for artistic mastery that transcends mere skill, reaching into the realms of the sublime. But beware the artist who becomes ensnared in the clutches of obsession, unable to put down the brush, sacrificing sleep, health, and relationships on the altar of a singular vision. The result may be a masterpiece, but at what cost? The canvas may be resplendent, but the life that painted it may be marred by shadows.

In the world of business, ambition is the driving force behind innovation and progress. Visionaries and entrepreneurs dare to dream big, to disrupt the status quo, and to reshape industries. They are fueled by a passion to make the world a better place, to provide solutions to problems, and to create value for society. Ambition in this context is a catalyst for economic growth, societal advancement, and human prosperity.

Yet, lurking in the corridors of corporate empires, obsession can also rear its head. Executives who obsessively pursue profit margins at any cost, ignoring the well-being of employees and the environmental impact of their actions, may achieve short-term success but sow the seeds of long-term disaster. The unbridled pursuit of wealth and power can lead to ethical lapses, corporate scandals, and the erosion of trust.

In the realm of love, ambition manifests as the desire for a deep and meaningful connection with another soul. It is the pursuit of a partnership founded on trust, respect, and mutual growth. Ambitious lovers seek not only personal happiness but also the fulfillment of their partner's dreams and aspirations. They understand that love is not a destination but an ongoing journey, an ever-evolving dance of two souls in harmony.

However, when love transforms into obsession, it becomes a suffocating force that smothers the flames of passion. The obsessed lover may become possessive, jealous, and controlling, unable to see their partner as an independent, autonomous being. They fixate on the object of their affection, neglecting their own well-being and happiness in a desperate bid to hold onto something that was never meant to be possessed.

In the pursuit of knowledge, ambition fuels the relentless quest for enlightenment. It drives scientists, philosophers, and thinkers to explore the mysteries of the universe, to unlock the secrets of existence, and to expand the boundaries of human understanding. Ambition in the realm of knowledge is a noble endeavor, one that enriches our lives, broadens our horizons, and propels us towards greater wisdom.

Yet, when the thirst for knowledge transforms into an unrelenting obsession, it can lead to the neglect of other aspects of life. The obsessed scholar may sequester themselves in isolation, forsaking human connection and the simple joys of life for the pursuit of esoteric truths. In their single-minded devotion to knowledge, they risk losing sight of the beauty and wonder of the world outside their books and experiments.

Consider, too, the athlete, driven by ambition to excel in their chosen sport. They train rigorously, honing their skills and pushing their physical limits, all in pursuit of victory and personal excellence. Ambition fuels their dedication, inspiring them to overcome obstacles and reach new heights of athletic prowess.

However, when this ambition becomes an all-consuming obsession, the athlete may push their body to the breaking point, risking injury and burnout. They may sacrifice their mental and emotional well-being in the relentless pursuit of success, neglecting the importance of balance and rest. The obsession with winning at any cost can lead to a hollow victory, devoid of the joy and fulfillment that should accompany such achievements.

In the domain of creativity, ambition is the muse that beckons artists, writers, and musicians to express their innermost thoughts and emotions. It inspires them to craft masterpieces that resonate with the human soul, to share their unique perspective with the world, and to leave an indelible mark on the annals of history. Ambition in the arts is a symphony of inspiration, dedication, and the ceaseless pursuit of creative excellence.

Yet, when ambition transforms into an unrelenting obsession with recognition and fame, it can stifle true artistic expression. The obsessed artist may compromise their vision to cater to popular trends, forsaking their authenticity for the sake of commercial success. They may become consumed by the pursuit of external validation, losing sight of the intrinsic joy of creation.

In the intricate dance of ambition and obsession, we find the very essence of the human experience. We are beings driven by desire, propelled by dreams, and shaped by our choices. It is in the delicate balance between these twin forces that we discover our true potential, our capacity for greatness, and our vulnerability to ruin.

Consider the astronaut, gazing at the stars with ambition in their heart. They embark on a perilous journey into the cosmos, driven by the desire to explore the unknown, to push the boundaries of human achievement, and to inspire generations to come. Ambition propels them beyond the confines of Earth, guiding their every move in the weightless expanse of space.

But should this ambition veer into obsession, the astronaut may become consumed by the isolation and danger of their mission. They may lose touch with the profound beauty of the universe, focusing solely on the mechanics of their tasks. The obsession to conquer the cosmos can lead to a sense of alienation from the very cosmos they sought to embrace.

In the realm of leadership, ambition is the force that compels individuals to take up the mantle of responsibility, to guide others towards a shared vision, and to make a positive impact on society. Ambitious leaders are driven by a sense of purpose, a commitment to ethical principles, and a vision of a better future for their followers.

However, when ambition transforms into a hunger for power and control, it can lead to tyranny and oppression. The obsessed leader may trample on the rights and well-being of others in their relentless pursuit of dominance. They may lose sight of the moral compass that should guide their actions, leaving a trail of destruction in their wake.

In the vast spectrum of human endeavor, ambition and obsession are the twin stars that illuminate our path. They are the yin and yang of our desires, the light and shadow that dance in perpetual motion. It is in the choices we make, the balance we strike, and the wisdom we cultivate that we determine whether our journey will be one of brilliance or ruin.

As we navigate the labyrinthine corridors of existence, let us heed the lessons of ambition and obsession. Let us embrace ambition as the guiding light that encourages us to reach for the stars, to aspire to greatness, and to pursue our dreams with unwavering determination. Let us recognize that ambition, when tempered by wisdom and balance, can lead us to heights we never thought possible.

Simultaneously, let us guard against the siren song of obsession, which can lure us into treacherous waters, blind us to the beauty of the journey, and lead us to a narrow, self-destructive path. Let us remember that obsession, unchecked and uncontrolled, can exact a heavy toll on our well-being, our relationships, and our humanity.

In the end, it is the choices we make, the equilibrium we maintain, and the harmony we seek that will determine the legacy we leave behind. Will it be a legacy of measured ambition, one that seeks excellence while honoring the holistic nature of our lives? Or will it be a legacy of unchecked obsession, one that may come at a great personal and societal cost?

In the end, we are the authors of our own stories, the painters of our own canvases, and the architects of our own destinies. It is in the delicate interplay of ambition and obsession that we craft the narrative of our lives—a narrative that, like a masterpiece of art, is defined by its balance, its wisdom, and its enduring beauty.

CHAPTER TWO

Confidence Unmasked: Navigating the Fine Line of Self-Belief

In the grand theater of human interaction, the characters of self-confidence and arrogance often step into the spotlight, casting their long shadows over the stage of our lives. This captivating drama unfolds as a testament to the intricacies of human behavior, revealing the intricate dance we perform each day. These two characters, self-confidence and arrogance, play a pivotal role in shaping the narratives of our existence.

Self-confidence, the virtuous protagonist of our tale, is a quiet, yet resolute force that emanates from within. It is the unwavering belief in one's capabilities, a gentle whisper that says, "I am capable." With self-confidence as the guiding star, individuals approach challenges with grace and determination. This character is rooted in a deep understanding of one's strengths and limitations, fostering a sense of self-worth that fuels personal growth and resilience. When self-confidence graces the stage, it inspires individuals to embrace opportunities, endure adversity, and treat life's hurdles as stepping stones on the path to self-improvement.

However, arrogance, the formidable antagonist, often masquerades as self-assurance but conceals a darker truth beneath its façade. It enters with an air of superiority, boldly proclaiming,

"I am superior," and frequently seeks to eclipse the brilliance of others. Arrogance fails to acknowledge the wisdom that can be gleaned from diverse perspectives, dismissing alternative viewpoints with disdain. It constructs barriers that isolate individuals from genuine connections and obstruct personal growth, all in the name of false self-importance.

Yet, the plot thickens as we delve further into this captivating narrative. There are instances when individuals who initially appear arrogant may harbor noble intentions and a genuine desire for self-improvement. Beneath the veneer of arrogance may reside valuable insights and hidden talents. Their seemingly haughty demeanor might serve as a shield against personal insecurities or as a manifestation of their fervent desire to catalyze positive change.

Consider, for example, the world of innovation and entrepreneurship. Here, fearless pioneers take center stage, armed with groundbreaking ideas and an unshakable belief in their power to reshape the world. However, this unyielding self-confidence can sometimes tiptoe perilously close to arrogance, leading to a disregard for alternative solutions and a failure to recognize the contributions of others. Unchecked arrogance has the potential to hinder progress and breed an atmosphere of isolation.

Nevertheless, it's essential to acknowledge that some of history's most exceptional innovators have exhibited shades of arrogance. Steve Jobs, the co-founder of Apple Inc., remains an iconic figure whose self-confidence was matched only by his demanding and, at times, dismissive nature. Yet, beneath the surface, it becomes evident that his overarching goal was not one of domination but of pushing the boundaries of technology and design. His arrogance, though occasionally off-putting, often mirrored his unwavering commitment to excellence.

In the realm of leadership, self-confidence can serve as a beacon that inspires teams to achieve remarkable feats. Leaders who believe in themselves and their vision have the power to motivate others to reach their full potential. However, this self-confidence can transform into arrogance if not tempered by humility. A leader who becomes impervious to dissenting voices or dismisses feedback as irrelevant can inadvertently lead their team down a perilous path.

A real-life illustration of this dynamic can be found in the remarkable story of Abraham Lincoln, one of America's greatest presidents. Lincoln possessed an unwavering self-confidence, yet he also exhibited the wisdom to surround himself with individuals who challenged his views. He encouraged robust debates within his cabinet, valuing the diversity of perspectives. This ability to balance self-confidence with humility allowed him to navigate the treacherous waters of the American Civil War and ultimately preserve the Union.

The fine line between self-confidence and arrogance casts a spotlight on the complexity of human nature and underscores the paramount importance of self-awareness and humility in our interactions. It teaches us that the demarcation between these two traits may be subtle, but their impact on our personal and professional lives is profound.

As we navigate this intricate dance between self-confidence and arrogance, it is imperative that we choose our steps with utmost care. By nurturing genuine self-confidence while taming the arrogance that threatens to overshadow our noble intentions, we can find harmony in our interactions with others. Ultimately, our role in the grand narrative of life is defined not by what we proclaim but by the authenticity of our character. It is in that authenticity that we discover the power to inspire, connect, and catalyze positive change.

In this visual tapestry of the human experience, self-confidence and arrogance stand as contrasting hues, each lending depth and complexity to the canvas of our lives. Imagine a striking illustration where self-confidence takes the form of a serene, unshakable tree, its roots firmly planted in the fertile soil of self-awareness. Its branches reach toward the sky, gracefully bending but never breaking in the face of adversity. The tree symbolizes growth, resilience, and the nurturing of one's inner strength.

In contrast, arrogance can be depicted as a formidable fortress, its towering walls constructed from bricks of self-importance. It stands proudly atop a hill, isolated from the surrounding landscape, its occupants oblivious to the wisdom that flows like a river beyond its gates. The fortress is an imposing presence, but its isolation leaves it vulnerable to the winds of change.

Within this artistic representation, imagine a scene where a young innovator, bathed in the warm glow of self-confidence, stands at the foot of the self-assured tree. With a humble heart and open mind, they reach out to the tree, seeking its shade and wisdom. The tree, with its branches offering shelter, symbolizes the synergy between self-confidence and humility—the perfect environment for growth and innovation.

On the other hand, picture a leader atop the fortress of arrogance, gazing out at a landscape devoid of other voices. The walls, though imposing, prevent them from hearing the echoes of dissenting opinions. In this solitary tower, the leader remains unaware of the vast landscape of collective wisdom that exists beyond their walls, a missed opportunity for enlightenment and progress.

In the portrayal of Abraham Lincoln, envision a powerful scene where he stands amidst a diverse group of advisors, each representing a different perspective. The room is vibrant with animated discussions, a kaleidoscope of ideas and viewpoints. Lincoln, with his self-confidence and humility interwoven like threads in a tapestry, presides over this assembly of minds, valuing each contribution and steering the nation through its darkest hours.

As the narrative unfolds, visualize a pivotal moment where the characters of self-confidence and arrogance engage in a delicate dance. They waltz together, their movements a testament to the balance that must be struck. Self-confidence leads with grace, while arrogance follows, gradually softening its edges. This dance represents the eternal struggle within us all—a struggle to harness the power of self-belief while remaining open to the wisdom of others.

In the grand finale, envision a stage bathed in a warm, golden light, where self-confidence and humility stand hand in hand, acknowledging their interdependence. They bow to the audience, a symbol of the harmony that can be achieved when these characters coexist in our lives. The audience, moved by this profound portrayal, leaves the theater with a deeper understanding of the intricate dance between self-confidence and arrogance, carrying with them the wisdom to navigate this eternal drama in their own lives.

In the end, the theater of human interaction is a stage where the characters of self-confidence and arrogance perform their roles with a mesmerizing blend of artistry and complexity. It is a stage where the audience, armed with the lessons of self-awareness and humility, can choose to applaud the virtuous lead or empathize with the deceptive antagonist. In this ongoing drama, we all play a part, and it is our choices that shape the narrative of our existence.

CHAPTER THREE

Freedom's Frontier: Striking a Balance between Independence and Anarchy

In the grand narrative of human society, the dichotomy between freedom and anarchy emerges as a captivating and perennial theme. On one hand, we have the noble concept of freedom—a beacon that guides our collective journey toward individual liberties, human rights, and self-expression. On the other hand, the specter of anarchy looms, casting a shadow of chaos, lawlessness, and societal breakdown. This narrative invites us to delve deep into the heart of governance, to examine the profound question of how we balance the inherent good of freedom against the undeniable dangers of anarchy.

Freedom, the virtuous protagonist of our tale, represents the innate human longing for self-determination and autonomy. It is the foundation upon which democratic societies are built, fostering an environment where diverse voices can be heard, where personal growth and self-expression are championed, and where innovation and creativity can thrive. In essence, freedom allows individuals to chart their own destinies, unfettered by oppressive constraints. It is the cornerstone of human rights and the embodiment of the pursuit of happiness. When nurtured and safeguarded, freedom empowers individuals to become active participants in shaping their own lives and, by extension, the world.

Contrastingly, anarchy, our menacing antagonist, is the embodiment of societal breakdown. It descends upon communities when the fabric of law and order unravels, leaving a vacuum of chaos and uncertainty. Anarchy emerges when individuals, in their pursuit of freedom, lose sight of the collective responsibility necessary to maintain a functioning society. It is the embodiment of unrestrained individualism, often characterized by a dangerous disregard for the well-being of others and the common good.

Yet, in the complex landscape of human affairs, we encounter a fascinating paradox. There are moments in history when individuals or groups, driven by noble intentions, walk a precarious tightrope, teetering on the edge of anarchy. These individuals might be animated by a fervent belief in the need for societal change or the rectification of long-standing injustices. Their agenda, rooted in the desire for positive transformation, can lead them to challenge established norms, even if it means treading close to anarchic territory.

Consider, for example, the Civil Rights Movement in the United States during the 1960s. Visionary leaders like Martin Luther King Jr. and Rosa Parks challenged the deeply entrenched racial discrimination that permeated American society. Their acts of civil disobedience were, at times, perceived as anarchic by those in power. Yet, their ultimate aim was not to plunge society into anarchy but to usher in an era of freedom and justice for all. Their struggle serves as a poignant reminder that the line between challenging the status quo and descending into anarchy can be perilously thin.

In the realm of technology and innovation, too, disruptive individuals and groups often find themselves at the intersection of freedom and anarchy. They challenge established industries, break regulatory barriers, and push the boundaries of what's possible. In doing so, they may be labeled as disruptors or even anarchists by some. However, their underlying agenda is to harness the power of freedom to drive progress and improve the lives of individuals.

The central challenge, then, becomes the responsible management of this intricate dance between freedom and anarchy. It necessitates robust governance, respect for the rule of law, and a collective commitment to the common good. As a society, we must recognize that while the pursuit of freedom is an honorable quest, it must be tempered by an acknowledgment of the need for order and shared responsibility.

In conclusion, the narrative of freedom versus anarchy challenges us to navigate a delicate balance. It underscores that the line between them is not always stark but often blurred by the complexities of human nature and societal dynamics. It calls upon us to safeguard our cherished freedoms while acknowledging that the path to a better world requires a nuanced equilibrium—one that allows individual liberties to flourish while maintaining the necessary structures and responsibilities to prevent anarchy from taking hold. In this balance, we find the promise of a society where freedom flourishes, where anarchy remains at bay, and where the true potential of humanity can shine.

As we traverse this narrative, we must also recognize the historical context that has shaped our understanding of freedom and anarchy. Throughout the annals of time, societies have grappled with these opposing forces, each leaving its indelible mark on the human story. From the ancient Athenian democracy, where the concept of citizen participation and individual rights began to crystallize, to the turbulent revolutions of the 18th and 19th centuries that sought to break the shackles of autocracy, the quest for freedom has been a driving force behind momentous change.

Yet, as history also reminds us, the unchecked pursuit of absolute freedom can lead to chaos. The French Revolution, with its radical fervor for liberty, equality, and fraternity, spiraled into the Reign of Terror, where anarchy reigned supreme, and the ideals of the revolution were tarnished by violence and excess.

In the modern era, the struggle between freedom and anarchy has taken on new dimensions. The advent of the internet and digital technology has ushered in an era of unprecedented access to information and communication. This digital frontier has given rise to both exhilarating expressions of freedom, where individuals can voice their opinions and connect with others across the globe, and disconcerting manifestations of anarchy, where misinformation and cybercrime threaten the fabric of society.

Moreover, the globalized world we inhabit presents us with a complex web of interconnectedness. While the idea of a borderless world fosters ideals of universal freedom and cooperation, it also raises concerns about how to maintain order and security in an environment where traditional boundaries are blurred.

In our quest to navigate the tension between freedom and anarchy, it is imperative that we draw upon the wisdom of philosophy, political theory, and the lessons of history. Thinkers like John Locke and Thomas Hobbes engaged in profound discourse about the social contract and the role of government in preserving order while safeguarding individual liberties. Their ideas continue to inform contemporary debates about governance and freedom.

Additionally, the notion of "negative" and "positive" freedom, as articulated by Isaiah Berlin, provides a framework for understanding the different facets of freedom. Negative freedom pertains to the absence of external constraints, allowing individuals to act as they please, while positive freedom concerns the capacity to achieve one's goals and desires. Balancing these two forms of freedom requires a delicate interplay between personal autonomy and the provision of opportunities and resources.

In the realm of art and literature, the struggle between freedom and anarchy has been a recurring theme. Countless works of fiction, from George Orwell's dystopian masterpiece "1984" to Aldous Huxley's "Brave New World," explore the consequences of a world where freedom is curtailed or unchecked. These literary endeavors serve as cautionary tales, reminding us of the fragility of societal order and the need to preserve our liberties with vigilance and responsibility.

The artistic world also offers a canvas for creative expression that challenges established norms and conventions. Avant-garde movements in art and music, such as Surrealism and Jazz, pushed boundaries and embraced the unconventional. While some critics viewed these movements as anarchic disruptions, they also celebrated the spirit of innovation and exploration that is intrinsic to human creativity.

In the arena of ethics, we confront profound questions about the limits of freedom and the ethics of responsibility. Philosopher Jean-Jacques Rousseau famously wrote, "Man is born free, and everywhere he is in chains." This statement encapsulates the tension between our innate desire for freedom and the constraints imposed by society. It prompts us to reflect on the ethical imperative of striking a balance between individual rights and the common good.

Religion, too, plays a role in our exploration of freedom and anarchy. Theological debates about free will, divine providence, and moral responsibility have shaped religious doctrines and influenced the course of history. Different faiths offer diverse perspectives on how individuals should exercise their freedom and whether there are divine laws that govern human conduct.

As we contemplate this grand narrative, we must also acknowledge that the world is in a state of constant flux. The challenges we face today, from climate change to global health crises, require us to reevaluate our understanding of freedom and anarchy in the context of a rapidly evolving world. These challenges demand international cooperation, shared responsibility, and innovative solutions that transcend traditional boundaries.

In the face of these challenges, we find ourselves at a crossroads. The narrative of freedom versus anarchy compels us to engage in thoughtful discourse, to cultivate empathy and understanding, and to seek common ground. It urges us to recognize that the preservation of freedom and the prevention of anarchy are not diametrically opposed goals but rather interconnected aspirations.

In conclusion, the grand narrative of freedom and anarchy is a timeless and intricate tale that continues to shape the course of human history. It is a narrative that challenges our intellect, stirs our emotions, and beckons us to consider the delicate balance between individual liberty and societal order. As we navigate this narrative, we must draw upon the wisdom of the past, engage with the complexities of the present, and envision a future where the promise of freedom can be realized while anarchy is kept at bay. In this ongoing story, we discover the profound potential of humanity to forge a path that celebrates both our individuality and our shared responsibility to build a just and harmonious world.

CHAPTER FOUR

Isolation Illuminated: Mastering Independence and Embracing Solitude

In the grand tapestry of human existence, the interwoven characters of independence and isolation emerge as captivating and intricate forces, each possessing its own distinct allure and carrying profound consequences. While on the surface, these two concepts might appear closely related due to their shared element of separation from others, they unveil vastly divergent outcomes and insights that intricately illuminate the complexities of our lives.

Independence, much like a virtuous protagonist in the epic of our lives, takes center stage. It embodies the spirit of self-reliance and autonomy, a reassuring whisper to individuals that declares, "You possess the capacity to chart your own course." Independence stands as the force that empowers people to pursue their dreams, make decisions aligned with their deepest values, and nurture a sense of self-worth deeply rooted in personal accomplishments. It encourages resilience and self-confidence, inviting individuals to embrace challenges as opportunities for growth and transformation.

Consider the young entrepreneur who embarks on the journey of creating a business from the ground up, their fervent commitment to independence propelling them forward. Navigating the intricate complexities of the business world, they make critical decisions and shoulder the weighty responsibilities of leadership with unwavering determination. This form of independence serves as an enduring source of inspiration and empowerment, not only driving personal success but also contributing significantly to the broader economic landscape.

On the contrary, isolation takes on the role of the antagonist in this narrative. It emerges as the character that shuns human interaction and withdraws into the shadowy realm of solitude, proclaiming with an air of defiance, "I am self-sufficient, and I need no one." While independence nourishes growth and resilience, isolation can breed a pervasive sense of loneliness and stagnation. At its most extreme, isolation can even lead to the profound alienation of individuals from the world, depriving them of the richness of human connections and the invaluable lessons that arise from them.

Yet, as any seasoned storyteller knows, the plot deepens when we delve into the nuances of isolation. In certain instances, individuals, driven by a sincere desire for personal growth or the pursuit of noble causes, may consciously choose to embrace a form of isolation as a means to an end. Picture the reclusive writer who retreats to a remote cabin to craft a literary masterpiece or the dedicated scientist who immerses themselves in solitude to unravel the mysteries of the universe. For them, isolation is not a symbol of detachment from humanity but rather a focused dedication to their craft, a deliberate choice to eliminate distractions and unearth the depths of their creative or intellectual potential.

Take, for instance, the renowned American author J.D. Salinger, best known for his literary masterpiece, "The Catcher in the Rye." He famously lived a reclusive life in rural New Hampshire. While his isolation from the public eye was conspicuously evident, it was not born of apathy or disdain for society. Rather, it represented a calculated decision to shield his private life from the intrusions of fame, preserving his creative sanctuary and enabling him to delve deeper into his art. Salinger's life story exemplifies how isolation, when harnessed with intent and purpose, can become a crucible for artistic brilliance.

The true challenge lies in discerning the fine line between purposeful independence and harmful isolation. For every J.D. Salinger, who harnessed his isolation to create literary masterpieces, there may be individuals who withdraw from society due to unresolved emotional scars, fear, or mistrust. Their isolation often perpetuates a cycle of loneliness and missed opportunities for personal growth. In such instances, isolation ceases to be a tool for self-improvement and becomes a stifling prison of one's own making.

The delicate equilibrium between independence and isolation underscores the intricate nature of human existence and emphasizes the paramount importance of self-awareness and intentionality in our choices. Independence, at its essence, should empower us to take charge of our lives while recognizing the intrinsic value of human connection. Isolation, when chosen, should serve as a deliberate instrument for self-discovery or as a means to advance a greater good, always with the door held ajar to rejoin the broader tapestry of life when the time is right.

In essence, independence, when tempered by an appreciation for human connection, possesses the capacity to lead to personal empowerment and a positive impact on society at large. Isolation, when wielded with purpose and a clear agenda, can act as a catalyst for profound discoveries and social change, casting its light on previously uncharted territories of knowledge and innovation.

As we reflect upon the intricate dance between independence and isolation, we are reminded that the choices we make possess the power to sculpt our destinies and shape the world around us. Our role in the grand narrative of life should not be defined solely by our moments of solitude but by the profound impact we create when we choose to emerge from it, carrying with us the lessons and wisdom of our independent journeys. Ultimately, it is through the harmonious interplay of these contrasting forces that we navigate the multifaceted complexities of our existence and discover our unique place in the ever-evolving human story.

CHAPTER FIVE

Hearts and Minds: The Empathy-Manipulation Conundrum

In the grand tapestry of human connections, empathy and manipulation stand as protagonists, engaged in a complex dance that unravels the intricate threads of genuine rapport and exploitative intent within our interactions.

Empathy, the virtuous lead, embodies the sublime art of not only comprehending but truly feeling the emotions of others. It grants us the ability to forge authentic connections, to step into the shoes of our fellow beings, and extend genuine support. It is the cornerstone upon which relationships are forged and nurtured, fostering trust and deepening the bonds that tie us together.

Yet, on the opposing side of this human stage, we find manipulation, the deceptive antagonist. This malevolent force dons many guises, all concealing its core desire to control, exploit, and gain an upper hand. It often shrouds its ulterior motives beneath the veil of empathy, using psychological stratagems to influence or deceive for personal gain, leaving the unsuspecting feeling used and betrayed.

The plot thickens when manipulation dons the disguise of righteousness, veiling itself under the banner of noble intentions. Individuals, swayed by their own sense of moral rectitude, might employ manipulative ploys in pursuit of what they perceive as the greater good. In these instances, manipulation masquerades as benevolence, yet its underlying motives clash fundamentally with the true essence of empathy.

Imagine a corporate setting where a colleague exudes an air of boundless empathy, offering unwavering support and guidance, seemingly propelled by a genuine desire to aid colleagues in surmounting their challenges. However, beneath this benevolent veneer, a manipulative agenda may be in motion. This individual might be leveraging their apparent empathy to curry favor with superiors, all while maintaining a façade of selflessness.

Now, let's shift our gaze to the political arena, a stage where the battle between empathy and manipulation plays out on a grand scale. Politicians often profess to champion the well-being of their constituents, asserting that their actions are propelled by empathy for the common good. However, some may resort to manipulative strategies to sway public sentiment, even if their intentions are rooted in what they perceive to be beneficial policies. This involves tactics such as exploiting emotions, disseminating misinformation, or instilling fear as a means to an end. This raises the profound question: Can a noble agenda ever justify manipulative means, or is the end never a fitting justification for the means employed?

Throughout history, leaders have emerged who manipulated public sentiment in pursuit of what they believed to be a greater good. Their visions, though often noble, led to calamitous consequences due to the manipulative methods they employed. The manipulation of emotions and beliefs, even when executed with seemingly positive aims, raises profound ethical questions about the means utilized and the potential for unintended fallout.

A vivid illustration from history is the civil rights movement in the United States, spearheaded by the iconic Dr. Martin Luther King Jr. Dr. King's unyielding dedication to justice and equality was deeply rooted in empathy. He endeavored to bridge racial chasms and eradicate discrimination through nonviolent means. His approach was marked by understanding, compassion, and the belief that love could vanquish hatred. In stark contrast, those who opposed him resorted to manipulative tactics, relying on fearmongering and hate speech to preserve the status quo. This stark contrast in approach underscored the power of empathy as a force for transformative change.

The struggle between empathy and manipulation serves as an evocative reminder that the distinction between these two forces can be subtle. It beckons us to scrutinize not only our actions but also the motives that underlie them. It compels us to discern the authenticity of our intentions and the ethicality of our methods.

In our daily interactions, as we navigate the labyrinthine network of human relationships, we must endeavor to embody genuine empathy while guarding against the seduction of manipulation, even when it disguises itself beneath the guise of a noble cause. This delicate equilibrium ultimately defines the essence of our character and our ability to forge connections, inspire trust, and contribute to a more compassionate and just world.

As we ponder this thought-provoking tableau of empathy versus manipulation, we are urged to cultivate a deeper understanding of ourselves and those who share our journey. Through this endeavor, we can navigate the intricacies of human interaction with authenticity, empathy, and an unwavering commitment to ethical conduct. In doing so, we forge a path towards a world imbued with compassion and justice, where the threads of genuine connection weave a tapestry of unity.

CHAPTER SIX

Tolerance Unveiled: Illuminating the Hidden Dilemma

In the intricate fabric of human relationships and societal dynamics, the interplay between tolerance and apathy presents us with a thought-provoking dilemma that invites us to explore the complex nuances of our responses to the world and its myriad challenges.

Tolerance, often celebrated as a cornerstone of empathy and open-mindedness, represents our ability to recognize and respect the diversity of beliefs, cultures, and perspectives that coexist in our global society. It's the glue that holds together the rich mosaic of human experience, promoting harmonious coexistence among individuals and communities with varying backgrounds and values. Tolerance encourages dialogue, invites the exchange of ideas, and fosters inclusivity—a vital foundation for a world striving for peace and understanding.

However, the question arises: can there be a shadow lurking beneath the virtuous surface of tolerance? Might it occasionally lead to unintended consequences or manifest as a façade for deeper issues? To explore this, we must navigate the delicate boundary between tolerance and its seeming opposite: apathy.

Apathy, generally perceived as a negative trait, occasionally conceals noble intentions. At its core, apathy can arise from a desire to detach from conflicts or divisive issues. Some argue that it can serve as a coping mechanism—a way to shield oneself from the emotional toll of engaging with seemingly insurmountable societal problems. In this interpretation, apathy becomes a self-protective response—a choice to avoid the emotional burden that often accompanies involvement in complex issues.

Consider, for instance, the tireless activists who dedicate their lives to championing a cause close to their hearts. These individuals often exhibit remarkable tolerance, engaging in constructive dialogue even with those who vehemently oppose their views. Yet, there comes a point where the relentless pursuit of a cause takes its toll, leading to burnout, emotional exhaustion, or even disillusionment.

In such instances, apathy might emerge as a defense mechanism—a way to regain emotional equilibrium. It can be viewed as a pause button, allowing individuals to step back temporarily, regroup, and protect their own mental and emotional well-being. In this light, what initially appears as apathy can be reinterpreted as an act of self-preservation, providing space for individuals to recharge before returning to their advocacy with renewed vigor.

However, it's crucial to tread carefully on this nuanced path, for apathy can quickly transform into complacency when noble intentions wane. In the realm of social justice, for example, apathy can become a substantial barrier to progress. When individuals disengage for an extended period, they risk allowing injustices to persist unchallenged.

To illustrate this, we can look to historical movements for civil rights and equality. Many of these movements encountered moments when activists, initially driven by an unwavering sense of justice, faced burnout and the emotional exhaustion of constant struggle. Some retreated momentarily, experiencing a temporary state of apathy. But, crucially, this apathy was meant as a respite rather than a permanent withdrawal. It was a strategic pause—a chance to rest and recover, to rekindle the flames of empathy and determination, before returning to the fight.

In the grand narrative of human existence, the interplay between tolerance and apathy urges us to reflect deeply on our responses to the world's myriad challenges. It encourages us to consider the intricate balance between understanding and detachment, empathy and self-preservation.

Ultimately, perhaps the true dilemma lies not in labeling one as inherently good and the other as inherently bad, but in recognizing that both tolerance and apathy have their moments of virtue and moments of potential peril. This recognition challenges us to explore the depths of our own motivations and to acknowledge the multifaceted nature of our responses to the world around us.

As we navigate this delicate dance, it is essential to strike a balance between the virtues of tolerance and the need for temporary apathy. It compels us to embrace the wisdom of knowing when to engage and when to take a step back for self-care, all while remaining steadfast in our commitment to a world where understanding and empathy prevail over indifference and division.

In the grand mosaic of human history, tolerance has often served as a beacon of hope, lighting the path towards a more harmonious and inclusive society. It has allowed diverse cultures to coexist, fostering an environment where people from various backgrounds can share their stories, beliefs, and traditions. Through tolerance, bridges are built between individuals, and empathy flourishes as people strive to understand one another.

Moreover, tolerance has played a crucial role in the advancement of human rights. It has been the driving force behind movements to end discrimination and prejudice, challenging societies to confront their biases and prejudices. Tolerance has paved the way for equality and justice, demanding that all individuals, regardless of their race, gender, or background, be treated with dignity and respect.

On the other side of this intricate interplay, we encounter apathy—an emotion often viewed with disdain. Apathy can manifest as indifference, disinterest, or a lack of motivation to engage with the world's challenges. Yet, there are moments when apathy takes on a different shade, one that reflects a need for self-care and preservation. It can be a lifeline for those who find themselves emotionally drained by the constant barrage of social and political issues.

Apathy can also serve as a reminder of the fragility of the human spirit. It underscores the importance of recognizing our own limitations and the boundaries of our emotional capacity. In the pursuit of noble causes, individuals can become overwhelmed, and apathy may be the body's way of signaling that it's time to pause and replenish one's emotional reserves.

To navigate the terrain between tolerance and apathy, we must appreciate the complexity of human emotions and motivations. It's not a binary choice between one or the other; rather, it's a delicate dance in which individuals must find their rhythm. Society benefits from both tolerance and moments of apathy, as they provide the necessary balance between engagement and self-preservation.

In examining this interplay, we must also acknowledge the ever-changing nature of societal challenges. What may have been a pressing issue yesterday might evolve or be replaced by new challenges tomorrow. This shifting landscape demands adaptability from individuals and communities, and it is within the folds of tolerance and occasional apathy that this adaptability can be found.

Furthermore, the interplay between tolerance and apathy reminds us of the importance of self-awareness. To effectively contribute to the betterment of society, individuals must be attuned to their own emotional states and needs. Recognizing when to step forward with tolerance and when to take a step back with measured apathy is a sign of emotional intelligence and resilience.

Ultimately, this interplay underscores the complexity of the human experience. It challenges us to recognize that there is no one-size-fits-all approach to engaging with the world's challenges. Instead, it calls for a nuanced understanding of ourselves and our place in the intricate tapestry of society.

In the grand symphony of human existence, tolerance and apathy are like the contrasting notes that create a harmonious melody. Tolerance represents the soaring crescendos of empathy and understanding, while apathy provides the soothing interludes of self-preservation and reflection. Together, they form a composition that speaks to the multifaceted nature of our responses to the world.

It's also important to acknowledge that the interplay between tolerance and apathy is not static; it evolves with time and circumstances. What may have been a moment of apathy can transform into renewed tolerance when individuals return to the fray with a fresh perspective and energy. In this way, apathy can be a catalyst for personal growth and transformation.

Moreover, the dynamic between tolerance and apathy serves as a reminder that societal progress is not a linear path. It's a journey filled with peaks and valleys, where moments of intense engagement are balanced by moments of respite. Just as nature follows the rhythm of seasons, human engagement with the world has its cycles, and apathy can be seen as a necessary part of this natural ebb and flow.

In conclusion, the interplay between tolerance and apathy invites us to delve into the intricate labyrinth of human emotions and responses. It challenges us to recognize that these two seemingly opposing forces can coexist and complement each other in our journey towards a more harmonious and just world. To navigate this complex terrain, we must cultivate self-awareness, adaptability, and a deep understanding of the ever-evolving challenges that shape our lives. In doing so, we can strike the delicate balance between tolerance and apathy.

CHAPTER SEVEN

Utopian Dreams: Navigating the Quest for an Ideal World

In the vast tapestry of human dreams and visions for a better world, idealism and utopianism emerge as two distinct yet interconnected threads. They both share a profound aspiration for improvement, a longing to transcend the status quo, but they traverse this journey with contrasting attitudes and, more significantly, disparate outcomes.

Idealism, the virtuous dreamer, embodies the belief that positive change is not only possible but can be achieved through diligent effort, persistent activism, and a profound sense of commitment. Idealism represents the tireless optimists, the champions of social justice, and the architects of progressive reforms. Think of the civil rights movement in the United States during the mid-20th century, where leaders like Martin Luther King Jr. and Rosa Parks embodied idealism at its finest. They held an unwavering belief that racial segregation and discrimination could be dismantled through nonviolent means and painstaking activism.

Contrastingly, utopianism, the beguiling visionary, envisions a world of absolute perfection—a utopia where every problem is solved, and every need is met. It declares, "Perfection is attainable," often with an almost messianic fervor. Utopianism paints a tantalizing portrait of an idyllic society, a paradise on earth, but in doing so, it frequently disregards the complexities and limitations inherent in human nature and society. Utopianism's allure lies in its promise of a world without pain, suffering, or injustice.

The tension between these two worldviews is most palpable when examining the realm of social change. Idealism compels individuals and movements to strive for a fairer society, to challenge inequalities, and to advocate for meaningful progress. It's the driving force behind legislative changes, grassroots activism, and the pursuit of equity. Yet, when idealism leans too heavily towards utopianism, it risks veering into the realm of unrealistic expectations and radicalism. The quest for rapid, sweeping change can sometimes lead to unforeseen consequences and disillusionment.

To illustrate this, we can revisit the civil rights movement in the United States. Idealism was at its core, as leaders like Martin Luther King Jr. and Rosa Parks pursued equality and justice through nonviolent means, pushing for incremental change within a deeply divided society. Their idealism was grounded in a sober understanding of the harsh realities of their time. They recognized that dismantling centuries-old systems of oppression required patience, persistence, and the forging of alliances across racial lines.

On the flip side, history offers glimpses of utopian experiments that faltered due to their lofty, impractical ideals. The Oneida Community, a 19th-century utopian experiment in communal living, sought to create a perfect society where individuals shared property and responsibilities. While the community had elements of idealism in its pursuit of a better world, it ultimately struggled to sustain itself due to the impracticality of its grand designs.

In the realm of technology and innovation, we witness the interplay between idealism and utopianism in the audacious goals set by visionaries like Elon Musk and Jeff Bezos. These individuals are idealists who believe in pushing the boundaries of what's possible through innovation and scientific advancement. They strive to solve critical global challenges, from space exploration to renewable energy, and their ventures have had a transformative impact on various industries.

However, the cautionary tale lies in the potential pitfalls of unchecked utopianism within technological innovation. The pursuit of a utopian ideal, in this context, could lead to the development and implementation of technologies with far-reaching consequences that may not have been adequately considered. Issues like privacy, ethics, and unintended societal impacts can become casualties of an overly optimistic utopian vision.

One of the most vivid examples of this cautionary narrative unfolds in the realm of surveillance technologies. While the development of advanced surveillance tools may promise security and efficiency, the unchecked pursuit of these technologies without ethical considerations can infringe upon individual privacy and civil liberties. The utopian ideal of a perfectly secure society must be tempered with a realistic understanding of the ethical dilemmas posed by such advancements.

In contrast, idealism in technological innovation seeks to address real-world problems pragmatically. Elon Musk's Tesla, for instance, aims to revolutionize the automotive industry by making electric vehicles more accessible and environmentally friendly. While this ambition is grounded in idealism, it acknowledges the need for practical solutions to combat climate change and create a sustainable future.

The delicate balance between idealism and utopianism serves as a poignant reminder of the complexity of human nature and the importance of self-awareness and humility in our pursuits. Idealism, when accompanied by pragmatism and a profound understanding of the multifaceted human condition, can be a driving force for meaningful change. It empowers us to take steps toward a better world while acknowledging the incremental nature of progress.

Utopianism, when harnessed with caution and a realistic perspective, can be a wellspring of audacious goals that inspire innovation and transformation. It invites us to dream big, to envision a world beyond the constraints of the present, but it also demands a tempered understanding of the potential pitfalls and challenges along the way.

In our ever-evolving world, the tension between these worldviews continues to shape our aspirations and the paths we choose to pursue them. The interplay of idealism and utopianism sparks innovation, challenges the status quo, and drives humanity forward. It reminds us that while perfection may remain elusive, the pursuit of a better world is a noble endeavor worthy of our collective efforts. This dynamic narrative of hope, tempered by reality, forms the crucible in which human progress is forged.

As we delve deeper into the realms of idealism and utopianism, it becomes evident that these contrasting philosophies also find resonance in the world of literature and art. Writers, poets, and artists have long grappled with these ideas, using their creative expressions to explore the boundaries of human aspiration.

In the realm of literature, idealism often takes the form of protagonists driven by a sense of moral duty and a desire to change their world for the better. Think of characters like Atticus Finch in Harper Lee's "To Kill a Mockingbird" or Jean Valjean in Victor Hugo's "Les Misérables." These literary figures embody the principles of idealism, standing as beacons of hope and moral rectitude in their respective narratives. Through their actions and convictions, they inspire readers to believe in the possibility of positive change, even in the face of adversity.

Utopianism, on the other hand, finds its literary expression in works that create meticulously crafted worlds where societal flaws are eradicated, and harmony prevails. Classic examples include Aldous Huxley's "Brave New World" and George Orwell's "1984." These dystopian novels serve as cautionary tales, warning against the dangers of unchecked utopian ideals. They depict societies where the pursuit of perfection has led to the suppression of individuality and freedom, underscoring the potential dark side of utopian visions.

In the realm of visual art, idealism and utopianism manifest in various forms. Idealistic art often portrays scenes of heroism, justice, and social progress. Think of paintings like "Liberty Leading the People" by Eugène Delacroix, which captures the spirit of the July Revolution in France. This masterpiece celebrates the ideals of freedom and equality, inspiring viewers with its portrayal of ordinary citizens rising to the occasion.

Utopian art, on the other hand, seeks to transport viewers to idyllic realms of perfection and harmony. The works of artists like Thomas Cole, known for his "The Course of Empire" series, depict idealized landscapes and civilizations, offering a glimpse into utopian visions of the past and future. These paintings invite us to contemplate the allure of utopia while raising questions about the sustainability of such paradises.

In the world of cinema, idealism and utopianism are recurring themes that captivate audiences. Films that explore idealistic narratives often revolve around characters who challenge the status quo and fight for justice. "Dead Poets Society," directed by Peter Weir, is a poignant example. The film follows an English teacher who inspires his students to question conformity and embrace the pursuit of their dreams. It resonates with viewers by celebrating the power of idealism to transform lives.

Conversely, utopian films transport us to realms of futuristic perfection or alternate realities where societal flaws have been rectified. "The Truman Show," directed by Peter Weir, offers a satirical take on utopianism as it portrays a man unknowingly living in a meticulously constructed, idealized world. The film raises thought-provoking questions about the nature of reality and the price of utopian ideals.

In conclusion, the dichotomy between idealism and utopianism runs deep in the tapestry of human thought and creativity. Whether in literature, visual art, or cinema, these philosophies serve as powerful lenses through which we examine the human condition, our aspirations, and the potential consequences of our dreams. Like two sides of the same coin, they remind us of the delicate balance between hope and reality, challenging us to navigate the complex terrain of progress and perfection with wisdom and humility.

CHAPTER EIGHT

Influence Intertwined: Leadership versus Authoritarianism

In the intricate theater of leadership, we are presented with two contrasting personas that often take center stage—the virtuous leader and the formidable authoritarian. These archetypes represent a profound and perpetual struggle for influence and power, with each carrying distinct qualities that hold the potential to mold the destinies of nations, organizations, and individuals.

Leadership, our virtuous protagonist, is a character of profound depth and complexity. It embodies qualities such as empathy, vision, and humility, serving as a beacon of inspiration and guidance. True leadership illuminates the path forward with a shared vision, orchestrating a symphony of cooperation that harmonizes diverse perspectives into a unified force. It is a force that seeks collaboration, treasures input from all quarters, and forges progress through consensus and shared values.

Contrastingly, authoritarianism stands as the formidable antagonist in this narrative. It is characterized by an unwavering grip on power, demanding obedience and ruling with resolute conviction in a singular agenda. Authoritarianism promises efficiency and order, but this often comes at the cost of individual liberties and the stifling of dissent. It is a character that brooks no challenge and tends to govern through coercion and fear.

Yet, paradoxically, within the shadow of authoritarianism, we often unearth a hidden layer. Beneath the stern facade, some authoritarian figures bear noble intentions and a sincere desire for order and progress. They believe that their assertive and forceful approach is necessary to combat chaos and drive transformative change. In their pursuit of control, they may aspire to bring stability and prosperity to their domain, even if it means employing authoritarian means to achieve these ends.

Consider the historical figure of Winston Churchill during World War II. Churchill's leadership style leaned heavily toward authoritarianism, yet his unwavering resolve and decisiveness played a pivotal role in rallying the British people during one of the darkest periods in their history. His leadership was marked by an unwavering commitment to protecting his nation's sovereignty and values, which, at times, necessitated a firm and authoritarian stance.

However, leadership, when stripped of its virtuous qualities, can devolve into a hollow form of influence. Leaders who succumb to the allure of power or lose sight of their moral compass may inadvertently perpetuate chaos and division. A leader who fails to listen to diverse viewpoints and collaborate effectively can become ineffective or even harmful.

A striking illustration of this pitfall can be found in the case of Theranos, a healthcare technology startup led by Elizabeth Holmes. Holmes possessed a vision for revolutionizing healthcare but became embroiled in scandal due to unethical practices. Her authoritarian approach stifled dissent and accountability, ultimately leading to the downfall of her once-promising company. This example underscores the dangers of authoritarianism when it lacks ethical principles and transparency.

Conversely, authoritarianism, when tempered by wisdom and a genuine commitment to the greater good, can achieve remarkable outcomes. History offers instances of leaders who, although wielding authority with a firm hand, were driven by noble intentions. They harnessed their power to effect transformative change and bring about progress.

In the corporate realm, effective leaders like Jeff Bezos of Amazon have displayed a balance between authoritative decision-making and fostering innovation. Bezos, while known for his demanding leadership style, also encourages experimentation and customer-centric thinking. This demonstrates how elements of both leadership and authoritarianism can coexist to drive innovation and growth within organizations.

Ultimately, the narrative of leadership vs. authoritarianism underscores the importance of a nuanced approach to wielding influence. Effective leaders must navigate the fine line between authoritative decisiveness and inclusivity, recognizing that genuine leadership involves not only achieving goals but also fostering unity, innovation, and the betterment of those they lead.

The battle for influence is an enduring one, and the outcome depends on the wisdom and character of those who step onto the stage of leadership. It is a complex and dynamic struggle, a narrative that continues to shape the destinies of nations, organizations, and individuals alike. In understanding the nuances of this battle, we gain insights into the profound impact that leadership, whether virtuous or authoritarian, can have on our world. The story unfolds with each new chapter, reminding us of the ever-present tension between these two archetypes in the theater of leadership.

CHAPTER NINE

Retribution Realities: Justice, Revenge, and the Maze Between

In the grand tapestry of human morality, the perennial struggle between justice and revenge stands as a compelling narrative, where the protagonists, although distinct in their motives and methods, share the common goal of righting wrongs. Justice, the virtuous luminary, epitomizes society's commitment to equity and fairness. It serves as the bedrock upon which our civilizational values are built, symbolizing the rule of law and the collective aspiration for a harmonious coexistence.

Justice is a structured guardian, its principles steeped in the notion of proportionality. It aspires to rectify wrongs through an impartial and systematic framework. It embodies the ideals of a balanced society, where wrongdoers face accountability within a framework that respects the sanctity of life and human dignity. When justice takes center stage, it symbolizes the triumph of reason, a triumph that transcends individual vendettas and upholds the greater good.

In stark contrast, revenge, the vengeful antagonist, emerges from the darkest corners of human emotion. It is born from pain and anger, whispering that the only path to healing is through the infliction of similar suffering upon the wrongdoer. Revenge is the embodiment of raw emotion and impulsive action. It often disregards the broader context and consequences, choosing instead the immediate satisfaction of settling scores.

Yet, within this timeless struggle lies a paradox. Justice, in its pursuit of fairness, occasionally finds itself ensnared in the web of bureaucracy and procedural rigidity. It may inadvertently perpetuate injustices through systemic flaws or fall short of meeting the emotional needs of victims seeking closure. In the world's courtroom dramas, justice sometimes appears to favor the clever over the just, leading to a sense of disillusionment among those who seek redress.

Conversely, revenge, while often painted in a negative light, may carry a noble agenda. It can be driven by a fervent desire to protect the vulnerable, to ensure that wrongdoers face consequences when formal systems fail to deliver. Revenge, in these instances, can become a desperate plea for accountability when justice appears distant, corrupted, or sluggish.

Consider the heart-wrenching stories of individuals who have lost loved ones to heinous crimes. Frustrated by lengthy legal processes, loopholes, and the potential for lenient sentences, they may take matters into their own hands. Their actions may blur the lines between these opposing forces. These individuals may not seek revenge for the sake of vengeance but rather for justice that seems perpetually elusive.

The pages of history are replete with examples where revenge was perceived as a necessary catalyst for change. The struggle for civil rights, for instance, was often marked by acts that some might label as vengeful. Activists, driven by a fervent commitment to rectify centuries of systemic oppression, sometimes employed confrontational tactics. In their eyes, these actions were not acts of revenge but rather urgent calls for justice and equality.

It is important, however, to heed the wisdom of Mahatma Gandhi, who famously cautioned that "an eye for an eye only ends up making the whole world blind." His words illuminate a profound truth: while revenge may momentarily appease the desire for retribution, it rarely leads to lasting solutions or societal healing.

In the world of international relations, the struggle between justice and revenge is epitomized by debates surrounding war crimes and acts of terrorism. Nations often grapple with the decision to pursue justice through legal channels or to succumb to the lure of revenge in the form of military retaliation. The choices made in these critical moments have far-reaching consequences, affecting not only the individuals directly involved but entire populations.

Yet, it is the delicate balance between these two forces that underscores the complexity of human nature. The eternal struggle between the innate human desire for retribution and the higher ideals of fairness and compassion forces us to confront our own moral compass.

In this unending clash between justice and revenge, the pivotal question we must continually ask ourselves is whether we can harness the raw energy of revenge and redirect it toward positive change or if we will allow it to perpetuate a cycle of pain and suffering. It is a question that transcends time and borders, reminding us that the choices we make in pursuit of justice define not only our own character but also the essence of the societies we create.

Consider, for instance, the Truth and Reconciliation Commission in post-apartheid South Africa. It was a remarkable endeavor that sought justice, not through revenge, but through a process of acknowledging past wrongs and promoting national healing. This initiative demonstrated that even in the most profound conflicts, a path toward justice and reconciliation can be forged without descending into the abyss of revenge.

As individuals and as societies, our actions in pursuit of justice should be guided by the principles of fairness, accountability, and the protection of human rights. Justice should strive to rectify wrongs while respecting the dignity of all parties involved. It should provide a beacon of hope for those who have suffered injustice, assuring them that their grievances will be heard and addressed within a framework that values the rule of law.

Ultimately, in the struggle between justice and revenge, it is the restraint of our baser instincts and the embrace of our higher ideals that lead to genuine progress. The moral complexities surrounding these forces underscore the profound journey of humanity, a journey that challenges us to continually seek a more just and compassionate world.

In the end, we must remember that justice is not merely an external system but a reflection of our shared values and aspirations. It is the embodiment of our commitment to building a world where righteousness prevails over retaliation, and where, in the words of Martin Luther King Jr., "Injustice anywhere is a threat to justice everywhere." Through our actions, we have the power to shape a world where justice, not revenge, prevails as the defining force in our human narrative.

CHAPTER TEN

Compassion's Conundrum: Balancing Forgiveness and Consequence

In the intricate landscape of human relationships, the dynamics between forgiveness and enabling stand as a complex, often paradoxical, interplay of emotional forces. At its core, forgiveness embodies the epitome of compassion and empathy, offering the promise of reconciliation, redemption, and the restoration of fractured bonds. Conversely, enabling, although rooted in noble intentions, possesses the potential to inadvertently become a patron of self-destructive behavior by shielding individuals from the repercussions of their actions.

Forgiveness, in its purest form, is a profound and liberating act. It transcends personal grievances and vindictiveness, allowing both the forgiver and the forgiven to unshackle themselves from the heavy burden of resentment and bitterness. It symbolizes the transcendence of hurt and the restoration of emotional equilibrium. The transformative power of forgiveness is its capacity to mend families torn apart by strife, rebuild trust eroded by betrayal, and offer a path forward after errors in judgment. It is the compassionate hand extended to raise others from the depths of their mistakes.

However, even forgiveness has its limits when it is wielded without discernment. In its unchecked benevolence, forgiveness can unwittingly metamorphose into enabling, which blurs the line between compassion and consequence. Enabling often manifests as a well-intentioned desire to shield loved ones from the harsh realities of life. While this intention may stem from a place of genuine care and concern, it can inadvertently create a protective bubble around individuals, shielding them from the natural consequences of their actions.

The essence of the challenge lies in the delicate equilibrium between forgiveness and enabling. Wisdom discerns when forgiveness serves as a catalyst for positive change, allowing individuals to reflect, grow, and mend their ways, and when enabling becomes a hindrance to personal development, perpetuating destructive behavior patterns. Compassion, when balanced with wisdom, is not about insulating others from life's lessons but about supporting them in their journey toward self-improvement.

This intricate balance is not always easy to strike. It necessitates the ability to navigate the complex terrain of human emotions, motivations, and intentions. It requires the wisdom to recognize when forgiveness should extend its soothing balm of healing and when enabling inadvertently prolongs the path to growth. True compassion, at its core, means holding individuals accountable for their actions while offering the possibility of redemption.

In practice, the dynamics of forgiveness and enabling often manifest within families, friendships, and close-knit communities. It is here that we frequently encounter the tension between the desire to nurture and protect our loved ones and the imperative of allowing them to confront the consequences of their actions. To strike this balance, one must grapple with the profound and challenging questions surrounding personal responsibility, accountability, and the complexities of human behavior.

The act of forgiveness, when guided by wisdom, fosters hope and renewal. It signals a willingness to move beyond the wounds of the past, to rebuild trust, and to provide individuals with the opportunity to mend their ways. In contrast, enabling, despite its well-intentioned nature, often prolongs the journey of self-discovery and growth. It inadvertently sends the message that accountability can be circumvented, diminishing the impetus for change.

Ultimately, the dance between forgiveness and enabling underscores the intricate nature of human existence. It serves as a reminder that our individual and collective journeys toward self-improvement are multifaceted and seldom linear. Within this interplay, we navigate the dualities that define the human experience, seeking the elusive equilibrium that fosters growth, compassion, and genuine healing. It is a continuous exploration, a profound reflection on the essence of our humanity, and an acknowledgment that the path to becoming better versions of ourselves involves both the grace of forgiveness and the transformative power of facing consequences with courage and resilience.

CHAPTER ELEVEN

Breaking Chains: Empowerment versus Overbearing Control

In the intricate interplay of human interactions, the dichotomy between empowerment and overbearing control represents a profound paradox. Both concepts are driven by fundamentally different motivations, yet they share a common thread – a desire to influence and mold the destinies of others. It is within the delicate balance of these contrasting forces that we find a thought-provoking examination of the dynamics that define human relationships and leadership.

Empowerment, with its inherently noble agenda, embodies the essence of fostering personal and collective growth in individuals. It is the act of equipping them with the necessary tools, knowledge, and opportunities to flourish autonomously. It is akin to tending a garden, where the soil is enriched, sunlight is abundant, and the seeds of potential are given ample room to sprout and grow. Empowerment uplifts, encourages, and nurtures a sense of self-efficacy.

Conversely, overbearing behavior, though it may occasionally originate from well-intentioned motives, frequently drifts into the realm of excessive control. It is analogous to tending a garden with an iron grip, where every aspect is meticulously regulated, stifling the very essence of natural growth. Overbearing individuals may believe they are guiding others toward what they perceive as the "right" path, but, in reality, they are inadvertently curtailing autonomy and impeding the realization of full potential.

The crux of this matter revolves around whether the end goal or the means employed in the pursuit of that goal holds greater significance. Empowerment embraces the fundamental principle that individuals have the right to choose their own paths, even if those paths diverge from what others may envision for them. It acknowledges that true strength lies in diversity, in recognizing the myriad ways people can flourish when provided the freedom to explore their unique journeys.

Conversely, overbearing behavior, despite its professed good intentions, often blinds individuals to their own latent potential. It assumes the role of dictation, stifling individualism, and imposing a singular vision upon others. It leaves minimal room for self-discovery, personal growth, or the development of autonomous decision-making skills.

Thus, as we navigate the complex terrain of empowerment and overbearing tendencies, it is imperative to reflect upon the essence of our actions. Are we genuinely empowering others by facilitating their independence and nurturing their self-belief, or are we inadvertently imposing our own desires, regardless of how benevolent they may be? The duality between empowerment and overbearing reminds us that the path to assisting others is often fraught with challenges, where the best of intentions can lead us astray.

Empowerment, as a concept, is grounded in the recognition of individuals as unique and capable beings. It thrives on the belief that personal growth is a deeply personal and self-directed endeavor. In an empowered environment, individuals are encouraged to take ownership of their choices and actions, fostering a sense of self-determination and accountability.

Such environments provide the fertile ground upon which creativity, innovation, and personal development can flourish. They grant individuals the freedom to explore their passions, to make mistakes, and to learn from them. Empowerment recognizes the intrinsic worth of each person's perspective and the potential for meaningful contributions from diverse viewpoints.

Contrastingly, the overbearing approach, while often well-intentioned, tends to subvert this notion of individual agency. It emerges from a desire to protect, to ensure success, and to guide individuals toward what is perceived as the "right" path. However, in doing so, it inadvertently undermines the very essence of self-discovery and self-reliance.

Overbearing behavior often results in a stifling environment where individuals feel a lack of autonomy and control over their own lives. It imposes external expectations and pressures, leaving little room for personal growth and exploration. In such circumstances, individuals may become dependent on external validation and direction, diminishing their ability to make informed decisions and take calculated risks.

The pivotal question in this discourse revolves around whether the end justifies the means. Empowerment, by its nature, advocates for the intrinsic worth and potential of each individual. It asserts that personal growth and development should be self-driven, with support and guidance serving as enablers rather than directives.

On the other hand, overbearing tendencies may justify their actions based on achieving a perceived greater good. However, they often disregard the fundamental principle that individuals have the right to make choices, even if those choices lead to failure or unconventional paths.

A nuanced understanding of empowerment recognizes that it involves not just providing opportunities but also fostering the skills and confidence necessary to navigate those opportunities effectively. It involves mentorship, guidance, and the creation of a supportive environment where individuals can learn and grow.

Overbearing behavior, despite its benevolent intentions, may inadvertently undermine individuals' confidence and problem-solving abilities. It can lead to a stifling environment where individuals feel compelled to conform to external expectations, inhibiting the development of critical thinking and decision-making skills.

In essence, empowerment seeks to elevate individuals by imparting the tools and knowledge needed for self-directed growth. It is rooted in trust, recognizing that individuals are best equipped to make decisions about their own lives. Overbearing behavior, conversely, operates from a place of control, where external guidance is considered essential for success.

It is vital to acknowledge that the line between empowerment and overbearing is not always clear-cut. In practice, individuals may experience a blend of both approaches, and the distinction can be context-dependent. Furthermore, individuals may respond differently to these approaches, with some thriving under empowerment and others feeling more secure with overbearing guidance.

In the realms of leadership and mentorship, striking a balance between empowerment and overbearing can be a significant challenge. Effective leaders recognize the importance of providing guidance and support while also allowing individuals the autonomy to make decisions and learn from their experiences.

Empowerment-driven leadership fosters a culture of trust, transparency, and collaboration. It encourages open communication and values diverse perspectives. In such an environment, individuals are more likely to take ownership of their work, engage in problem-solving, and contribute creatively to organizational goals.

Conversely, leaders who adopt an overbearing approach may inadvertently stifle creativity and innovation within their teams. By exerting excessive control and micromanaging, they discourage independent thinking and problem-solving. This can lead to a workforce that is dependent on constant direction, diminishing its ability to adapt and thrive in dynamic environments.

The implications of these approaches extend beyond the realm of leadership and mentorship. They influence the dynamics of personal relationships, parenting, education, and even societal structures. Recognizing the consequences of empowerment and overbearing behaviors is essential in fostering healthy, thriving communities and organizations.

In the context of education, for instance, an empowerment-driven approach encourages students to take an active role in their learning. It emphasizes critical thinking, creativity, and problem-solving skills. Educators serve as facilitators and guides, empowering students to explore their interests and develop a sense of ownership over their education.

On the contrary, an overbearing educational approach may prioritize standardized testing and rigid curricula over individualized learning experiences. It can stifle students' curiosity and creativity, leaving them ill-prepared to adapt to the complexities of the real world.

In parenting, a similar dynamic emerges. Empowerment-oriented parents aim to raise self-reliant, confident children who can navigate life's challenges independently. They encourage open communication, active decision-making, and the development of a strong sense of self.

Overbearing parents, while driven by a desire to protect their children, may inadvertently hinder their growth. By exerting excessive control and making decisions on their behalf, they may deprive children of opportunities to develop essential life skills and decision-making capabilities.

Society at large also grapples with the balance between empowerment and overbearing control. Democratic societies, for instance, emphasize individual freedoms, personal choice, and autonomy. They recognize that empowering individuals to make informed decisions about their lives is essential for social progress and personal fulfillment.

However, societies that lean toward overbearing control may curtail individual freedoms and prioritize conformity and uniformity. Such environments can limit personal expression and hinder social progress, as they may resist change and innovation.

Navigating the complexities of empowerment and overbearing in these various contexts necessitates a nuanced and thoughtful approach. It requires individuals, leaders, and institutions to reflect on their motives and actions critically. It also calls for a recognition of the potential consequences of these approaches on individuals' autonomy, growth, and well-being.

In conclusion, the duality between empowerment and overbearing is a profound reflection of the human experience. It reminds us that the means by which we seek to influence and guide others can have a profound impact on their growth, independence, and sense of self. Whether in leadership, education, parenting, or societal structures, the delicate balance between empowerment and overbearing is a critical consideration that shapes the fabric of our relationships and communities.

Striking this balance is not a static endeavor but an ongoing process that requires adaptability, empathy, and a deep understanding of the unique needs and aspirations of individuals. It calls for an approach that values autonomy and personal growth while recognizing the importance of support and guidance in the journey toward self-fulfillment and collective progress.

CHAPTER TWELVE

Belief's Spectrum: Navigating Hope and Denial

In the intricate tapestry of human emotions, few threads are as entangled as hope and denial. At first glance, they may appear to be birds of the same feather, both associated with a certain degree of optimism about the future. However, beneath the surface, they represent two divergent approaches to dealing with life's challenges, with profoundly different intentions and consequences.

Hope, in its essence, is a powerful force. It is the beacon that guides us through the darkest of storms, illuminating the path forward even when the world seems shrouded in darkness. Hope acknowledges the difficulties and obstacles before us, but it refuses to surrender to despair. It is the spark that ignites our resilience, allowing us to confront adversity with unwavering determination.

This optimistic outlook does not spring from naiveté but rather from a deep-rooted belief in the possibility of better days. Hope instills in us the conviction that change is attainable, that efforts are not in vain, and that the human spirit can prevail. It is, in essence, a catalyst for action. Hope inspires us to innovate, to create, to strive for a brighter future not only for ourselves but for all of humanity.

Conversely, denial, although superficially resembling hope, represents a perilous descent into self-deception. It is the act of consciously or unconsciously evading harsh realities and uncomfortable truths. Denial blinds us to the weighty issues that demand our attention, rendering us incapable of confronting the real challenges that beset us.

Denial might provide temporary solace, a fleeting reprieve from the discomfort of facing difficult truths. It is akin to the ostrich that buries its head in the sand while danger looms. This psychological defense mechanism seeks refuge in the familiar, rejecting the notion that change is necessary or even possible.

However, the most critical disparity between hope and denial lies not in their surface resemblance but in their underlying agendas. Hope, as the benevolent guide, is inherently forward-looking. It seeks positive change and transformation. It empowers us to act, to make a difference, and to shape the course of our lives and our world.

On the contrary, denial, with its illusory comfort, often has an agenda that is passive and regressive. It clings to the status quo, refusing to acknowledge that change is not only beneficial but, in many cases, imperative. It is an impediment to progress, allowing problems to fester and deepen rather than seeking resolution.

One profound example of hope's transformative power can be observed in social movements. Throughout history, hope has been the driving force behind movements for civil rights, gender equality, and environmental conservation. It is hope that mobilizes individuals and communities to challenge the established order, to demand justice, and to push society towards positive change.

Conversely, denial can be seen as a stumbling block, especially in addressing urgent global challenges. Take, for instance, the issue of climate change. Climate denial, born out of a refusal to accept the reality of anthropogenic global warming, has impeded international efforts to mitigate its effects. By clinging to denial, individuals and entities undermine the necessary collective actions to combat this existential threat.

Furthermore, in the realm of public health, the COVID-19 pandemic serves as a stark illustration of the consequences of denial. The initial denial of the virus's severity and the subsequent resistance to public health measures hindered effective responses and, tragically, led to preventable loss of life.

Hope is not merely a passive sentiment; it is an active force that compels us to envision a better world and work towards its realization. It inspires innovation, fuels progress, and emboldens us to confront challenges head-on.

Conversely, denial, with its illusory comfort, encourages a dangerous passivity. It allows us to bury our heads in the sand, hoping that problems will magically disappear. It is the short-term reprieve that ultimately yields long-term consequences.

In essence, hope embodies the unwavering belief in a brighter future, tempered by realism and the willingness to act. It is a dynamic force that has the power to transform our lives and our world.

Denial, on the other hand, offers the transient solace of ignorance. While it may momentarily shield us from discomfort, it does so at the expense of progress, perpetuating problems and postponing their resolution.

As we navigate the spectrum between hope and denial, it is imperative to recognize that hope, not denial, holds the key to our collective betterment. It calls us to embrace ambiguity and uncertainty, to question the boundaries of what is possible, and to engage in a lifelong conversation with the dualities that define the human experience.

Let us remember that hope is not the absence of adversity; rather, it is the unwavering belief that we can overcome it. It is the force that urges us to confront the challenges of our time, from social injustices to environmental crises, with courage, determination, and a collective commitment to a better future.

In conclusion, hope is the compass that guides us through the labyrinth of life, pointing us towards the light even in the darkest of hours. Denial, on the other hand, is the siren's call that lulls us into complacency, only to lead us astray in the end. As we explore the intricacies of these contrasting states of mind, may we embrace hope as the catalyst for change, the catalyst that propels us toward a brighter and more promising horizon.

CHAPTER THIRTEEN

The Fire Within: Passion versus Fanaticism

In the intricate landscape of human behavior and motivation, passion and fanaticism are two forces that stand as exemplars of unwavering fervor. Yet, their outcomes diverge dramatically, like two paths branching from the same origin. While both can elicit extraordinary dedication, the distinctions between them are critical, and understanding these distinctions is pivotal for navigating the fine line between constructive enthusiasm and destructive extremism.

Passion, the elder sibling, is akin to a steady flame, radiating warmth and illumination. It is the catalyst that drives individuals to push the boundaries of creativity, knowledge, and societal progress. When passion is at the helm, it operates in harmony with reason and responsibility. It manifests as an artist's dedication to honing their craft with precision, a scientist's tireless quest for scientific discovery, or an activist's unwavering commitment to humanitarian causes. This form of passion is deeply rooted in genuine curiosity, the pursuit of excellence, and a desire to contribute positively to the world.

On the contrary, fanaticism, the younger, impulsive sibling, appears deceptively similar. It can also emanate a fervent glow, but this intensity is often unguided, unchecked by reason, and susceptible to extremist tendencies. Fanaticism can manifest as an uncompromising attachment to an ideology or cause, often resulting in intolerance, violence, and the undermining of individual liberties. It is akin to a wildfire, consuming all in its path without discrimination, leaving a scorched earth in its wake.

At the heart of this discussion lies the question: What distinguishes passion from fanaticism? The answer, it seems, lies in the realms of balance and perspective. Passion, when coupled with reason, transforms into a formidable force for progress. It is the engine that propels innovators, artists, and advocates toward their goals. It channels creativity and commitment into tangible, beneficial outcomes. It drives us to learn, to create, and to make our world a better place.

Fanaticism, however, emerges when this passionate drive loses its compass. It occurs when individuals become blinded by their fervor, when they forsake empathy and critical thinking in favor of an unbending adherence to their chosen ideology. It's the transformation from a passionate advocate for social change to a militant extremist, willing to resort to violence to further their cause.

The spectrum between passion and fanaticism is wide, and the transition from one to the other can be subtle. So how do we navigate this complex territory?

The key, it seems, lies in balance and discernment. True passion, guided by reason, is the driving force behind the world's most profound innovations and positive transformations. It is the fuel that powers change-makers and visionaries, inspiring them to persevere in the face of adversity.

At the same time, unchecked passion can give way to fanaticism when individuals lose the capacity for self-reflection, compromise, and empathy. It is the passionate artist who becomes so obsessed with perfection that they alienate those around them, the activist who loses sight of peaceful means in the pursuit of their agenda, or the scientist who becomes dogmatic in their theories, ignoring dissenting evidence.

The world has been shaped by passionate individuals who have harnessed their fervor for good. They have challenged the status quo, broken down barriers, and achieved remarkable feats. Think of the civil rights activists who fought tirelessly for equality, the scientists who tirelessly researched cures for diseases, and the artists who created timeless works of art that continue to inspire.

However, history is also marked by instances of unchecked fanaticism, where passion, untempered by reason and empathy, has led to catastrophic consequences. Think of religious conflicts, political extremism, or social movements that have spiraled into violence and oppression.

In the perpetual tussle between passion and fanaticism, the ultimate victor is discernment. It is the capacity to harness the intensity of passion while simultaneously restraining the flames of fanaticism. Discernment enables individuals to remain grounded, to critically evaluate their beliefs and actions, and to adapt when necessary.

To cultivate discernment, we must be vigilant. We must continually question our own motives and ideologies, seek out diverse perspectives, and remain open to the possibility that we may be wrong. We must remember that passion is not inherently destructive, and fanaticism is not the inevitable consequence of fervor. Instead, it is our responsibility to steer our passions toward constructive ends, to use our intensity to inspire, educate, and uplift.

In conclusion, the dichotomy between passion and fanaticism serves as a profound reminder of the power and complexity of human motivation. Both have the potential to shape the world, but the path they tread is determined by our choices and our ability to wield them responsibly. The flames of passion may burn brightly, but it is our capacity for discernment that ensures they illuminate rather than incinerate the path ahead.

CHAPTER FOURTEEN

Daring Deeds: Navigating Risk-taking and Foolhardiness

In the complex landscape of human endeavor, the distinction between risk-taking and foolhardiness is akin to treading a fine line between success and catastrophe. These two concepts share common ground in their audacity to venture beyond the familiar, yet their outcomes diverge dramatically due to differences in approach and mindset.

At its core, risk-taking is a calculated act of courage. It is the willingness to embrace uncertainty and step into the unknown, driven by a vision of potential rewards. This character, "Risk-Taking," envisions a future where calculated chances can lead to growth, innovation, and progress. This character acknowledges that life's greatest achievements often require stepping out of one's comfort zone and confronting the unfamiliar.

Contrastingly, "Foolhardiness" is characterized by an audacious but impulsive disposition. It embodies a reckless approach to challenges, driven by bravado rather than reason. This character charges ahead without due diligence, often blinded to potential pitfalls. While it may be well-intentioned, foolhardiness lacks the restraint and strategic thinking that characterize prudent risk-taking.

The crucial distinction between these two concepts is rooted in their approaches. Risk-taking approaches uncertainty with a respect for its unpredictability. It involves diligent preparation, strategic planning, and a willingness to adapt when faced with adversity. In essence, it is an informed gamble, guided by a calculated assessment of potential outcomes.

Foolhardiness, on the other hand, is characterized by a disregard for the complexities of uncertainty. It charges forward with an unwavering belief in its invincibility, often ignoring warning signs and consequences. It may indeed possess noble intentions but lacks the wisdom to differentiate audacity from recklessness.

The key question, then, is how to distinguish between these two characters in the narrative of our lives. To navigate this fine line successfully, we must cultivate a deep well of wisdom and discernment. This discernment arises from a profound understanding of our objectives and the consequences our actions may yield.

In our own life stories, we each assume the roles of playwright and protagonist. The characters of risk-taking and foolhardiness await our direction. By carefully weighing the risks and rewards, we can make informed decisions that lead to personal and professional growth. This path, guided by calculated courage, transforms life's challenges into opportunities for achievement.

In essence, risk-taking, when executed with prudence, is the vehicle of progress. It embodies the audacity to dream, the courage to act, and the resilience to endure setbacks. It fosters innovation, encourages exploration, and fuels the pursuit of excellence. True risk-takers do not shy away from adversity but rather embrace it as a crucible for growth.

Conversely, foolhardiness, despite its zeal, can lead to missteps and missed opportunities. It may be propelled by noble intentions but is often undone by its inability to recognize the importance of strategic planning, informed decision-making, and humility in the face of uncertainty.

The lessons we can glean from this duality are profound. Firstly, we must acknowledge that the line separating risk-taking from foolhardiness is subtle, and its boundaries shift with context. Secondly, to navigate this line effectively, one must hone their ability to discern between audacious but calculated ventures and reckless bravado.

In this era of rapid change and innovation, calculated risk-taking is a cornerstone of success. It encourages individuals and organizations to innovate, to venture into uncharted territories, and to adapt to evolving landscapes. It thrives on the understanding that failure, while possible, is not the end but a stepping stone towards growth.

Contrarily, foolhardiness jeopardizes both personal and collective progress. It can lead to unnecessary risks, financial loss, and tarnished reputations. It is often marked by a refusal to acknowledge warning signs or a failure to learn from past mistakes.

Ultimately, our capacity to differentiate between these two concepts and embrace prudent risk-taking can significantly influence the course of our lives. It is a skill that requires continuous honing, self-reflection, and a willingness to embrace uncertainty as a canvas for achievement.

In conclusion, risk-taking and foolhardiness may share audacity, but they diverge profoundly in their approaches and outcomes. The former, guided by wisdom and informed decisions, leads to personal and professional growth. The latter, fueled by impulsivity and a disregard for consequences, can result in recklessness and missed opportunities.

As we navigate the ever-changing landscapes of our lives, let us recognize that the choice between these characters lies within us. With careful consideration, we can embrace the audacious spirit of risk-taking while tempering it with wisdom and discernment. In doing so, we transform life's uncertainties into opportunities for personal and collective advancement.

CHAPTER FIFTEEN

Honesty's Heartbeat: Striking the Delicate Balance

In the realm of ethical values, honesty reigns supreme as a pillar of integrity and transparency. The fundamental principle of honesty is rooted in the unequivocal commitment to telling the truth, even when faced with uncomfortable or challenging circumstances. In its purest form, honesty serves as the bedrock of trust, forming the basis of genuine and meaningful human relationships. It is a beacon guiding individuals and societies toward ethical behavior, accountability, and the pursuit of truth.

However, within the concept of honesty, a paradoxical tension often emerges—the distinction between honesty and what is colloquially termed "brutal honesty." At its core, brutal honesty involves an unapologetic commitment to truthfulness, unvarnished by diplomacy or consideration of emotional consequences. It presents a challenging question: Can unwavering truthfulness sometimes be detrimental, undermining the very principles it aims to uphold?

On one hand, honesty serves as a vital catalyst for personal growth and societal progress. When wielded with empathy and care, honesty can be a constructive force for individuals, allowing them to confront their weaknesses, accept responsibility for their actions, and initiate personal development. In the broader context, honesty enables open and authentic dialogues, fostering trust and understanding among diverse communities. In situations of conflict, honesty paves the way for reconciliation, conflict resolution, and lasting solutions.

Yet, on the other side of this dualistic spectrum lies the notion of brutal honesty—an approach that leaves no room for tact, diplomacy, or emotional sensitivity. The foundation of brutal honesty is stark and unyielding: the unfiltered, unapologetic, and often abrasive delivery of the unvarnished truth. In its pursuit of absolute transparency, brutal honesty can inflict harm, alienate individuals, and create unnecessary discord. It disregards the emotional impact of its words, sometimes causing more pain than the issues it aims to address.

Consider, for instance, a situation where a friend seeks your opinion on a personal matter. Honesty would advise providing feedback with compassion, highlighting positive aspects while gently suggesting areas for improvement. Brutal honesty, in contrast, might manifest as a curt and unsparing declaration: "This is terrible." While the latter may undeniably convey the truth, it does so without regard for the emotional well-being of the recipient, potentially causing lasting harm.

The complexity of this duality becomes evident when we ponder the balance between these two facets of honesty. Is it possible to remain true to the principles of truthfulness while recognizing the profound importance of kindness and empathy in our interactions? Can we harmonize the pursuit of truth with the preservation of emotional well-being?

Perhaps the solution lies in the realm of compassionate communication—a nuanced approach that merges honesty with empathy. Honesty, when complemented by sensitivity, can catalyze personal and collective growth. It prompts us to acknowledge that the intent behind our words is as significant as the words themselves. The practice of being honest without resorting to brutality calls for the consideration of not only what we say but also how we deliver our truths.

In this context, honesty becomes a powerful tool for both introspection and interpersonal connection. It urges individuals to navigate the intricate web of human interaction with empathy and wisdom, recognizing the profound implications of their words on others. It compels us to ponder our ethical responsibility in wielding the power of truth.

The dichotomy of honesty vs. brutal honesty serves as a profound lens through which to examine the complexities of human relationships and ethical behavior. It prompts us to reflect upon our role in these interactions, encouraging us to contemplate when to be honest and when to be gently truthful. It reminds us that, while the truth has the capacity to liberate and strengthen, it is our approach to truth that ultimately defines the quality of our relationships and the impact we have on those around us.

Therefore, as we navigate the nuances of this dualistic concept, let us aspire to cultivate a world where honesty is not a blunt instrument but a compassionate and guiding force. Let us strive for a world where the pursuit of truth coexists harmoniously with the preservation of kindness, where individuals possess the wisdom to discern when to be honest and when to deliver their truths with a gentle touch.

In conclusion, the exploration of honesty vs. brutal honesty invites us to embark on a profound journey of self-discovery and ethical introspection. It reminds us that our actions, even those as seemingly straightforward as speaking the truth, can have profound consequences on the human experience. It encourages us to recognize that in the delicate balance between honesty and empathy, we can discover the path to more meaningful, compassionate, and harmonious relationships.

CHAPTER SIXTEEN

Faith Explored: Navigating Belief and Blind Faith

In the intricate tapestry of human existence, the juxtaposition of faith and blind faith emerges as a profound and often contentious duality. These two concepts, while sharing a common origin, lead to divergent destinations when it comes to belief systems and their implications in our lives.

At its core, faith represents a source of comfort, strength, and guidance for countless individuals. It serves as the bedrock upon which people build their moral and spiritual frameworks. Faith is the beacon of hope in times of despair, the unwavering trust in something larger than oneself, whether that be a divine presence, a collective cause, or the intrinsic goodness of humanity. It inspires people to act altruistically, fosters community bonds, and drives them to strive for noble goals.

On the other hand, blind faith represents a dangerous departure from this profound sense of trust and guidance. It is the uncritical acceptance of beliefs without room for questioning, analysis, or introspection. Blind faith can lead individuals down a perilous path where they willingly relinquish their capacity for rational judgment in favor of rigid adherence to a particular ideology or doctrine. In such instances, it ceases to be a source of enlightenment and becomes instead a tool for fanaticism, intolerance, and even cruelty. It erects impenetrable barriers to scrutiny and critical thinking.

The key to navigating this intricate duality lies in the art of discernment. Authentic faith encourages individuals to embark on an intellectual and spiritual journey. It urges them to explore the depths of their beliefs, to question, and to seek understanding. It invites humility, the recognition that human comprehension is limited, and that the universe's mysteries may be beyond full human grasp. Genuine faith, therefore, is not threatened by doubt or inquiry; rather, it thrives upon them, as they serve as vehicles for deeper spiritual insight.

In contrast, blind faith discourages questioning and inquiry, thereby undermining the very essence of faith itself. It can result in a mindset that is impervious to new information, resistant to change, and dismissive of alternative perspectives. This form of belief often rests upon an unwarranted assumption that one's particular belief system is infallible, leading to a dogmatic and rigid worldview.

In a world where our beliefs can shape not only our individual actions but also the collective destiny of humanity, the distinction between faith and blind faith takes on profound ethical significance. It compels us to cultivate faith that is rooted in compassion, empathy, and the quest for truth. True faith, with its humility and willingness to seek understanding, encourages dialogue and bridge-building between disparate belief systems, fostering peace and cooperation. It promotes critical thinking, allowing individuals to distinguish between what is worthy of belief and what is not.

Conversely, the treacherous path of blind faith stifles such growth and self-reflection. It can lead to divisiveness, as individuals are more likely to perceive those who hold differing beliefs as threats rather than as fellow seekers of truth. It discourages the open-mindedness necessary for moral and intellectual progress.

To guard against the dangers of blind faith, it is incumbent upon individuals and societies to cultivate a culture of inquiry and intellectual honesty. This involves nurturing an environment where questions are not met with hostility but are embraced as opportunities for growth. It entails recognizing that human knowledge is continually evolving, and our beliefs should be open to adaptation in the light of new information.

Moreover, it is essential to differentiate between faith and fanaticism. Fanaticism often masquerades as faith, but it is characterized by an unwillingness to entertain any perspective other than its own. Genuine faith, on the other hand, can withstand scrutiny and welcomes dialogue. It acknowledges the inherent limitations of human understanding while seeking to transcend them.

In the pursuit of authentic faith, it is also crucial to appreciate the diversity of belief systems that exist in our interconnected world. Each belief system represents a unique facet of the human experience, and while they may differ in details, many share common threads of compassion, justice, and love. Encouraging dialogue and mutual respect among diverse belief systems can foster greater understanding and harmony in a pluralistic world.

It is a testament to the complexity of the human condition that faith and blind faith can coexist within the same individual or society. This juxtaposition underscores the ongoing struggle between our innate capacity for reason, empathy, and self-awareness, and the seductive allure of unwavering certainty and simplicity offered by blind faith.

Ultimately, the choice between faith and blind faith is a deeply personal one, a reflection of our own values, character, and worldview. It is a choice that shapes not only our individual destinies but also the world we collectively create. In this journey of exploration, may we continually seek the light of authentic faith, recognizing that it is through the interplay of our beliefs, our questions, and our shared humanity that we uncover the profound truths that define our existence.

CHAPTER SEVENTEEN

Progress Unraveled: Balancing Innovation and Prudence

In the landscape of human progress, innovation stands as the beacon guiding us forward. It represents our collective yearning to transcend limitations, shatter boundaries, and reach new horizons. Yet, as we traverse this uncharted territory, there exists a formidable adversary: recklessness. The struggle between innovation and recklessness is a profound one, characterized by the delicate balance between daring advancement and heedless abandon. It is a narrative that has played out in the annals of history, illustrating the critical importance of prudence in our pursuit of progress.

Innovation is the driving force behind our ever-evolving world. It propels us into the future, fueling technological breakthroughs, scientific discoveries, and societal transformations. It encourages us to question the status quo, embrace change, and envision a world that goes beyond the boundaries of our current understanding. Innovation is the embodiment of human curiosity and ingenuity, offering the promise of a brighter, more efficient, and more inclusive future.

However, in the relentless quest for innovation, there lies the peril of recklessness. Recklessness manifests as an unbridled pursuit of progress without due consideration for the potential consequences. It often involves a disregard for ethical principles, neglect of long-term sustainability, and a cavalier attitude toward the collateral damage that can result from unchecked innovation. It is the perilous journey into uncharted waters without a compass or a map, driven solely by the thrill of exploration.

Consider the rivalry between two automotive pioneers, Henry Ford and Karl Benz. Ford's innovation, the assembly line, revolutionized the production of automobiles, making them accessible to the masses. His approach, while groundbreaking, was underpinned by a practical ethos. It aimed not just to create something new but to transform society by making cars affordable and accessible to ordinary people.

Karl Benz, the inventor of the first gasoline-powered car, can be seen as a more audacious innovator. His early experiments were pioneering, but they were also expensive and extravagant. It took Ford's pragmatism to refine and popularize the automobile. Benz's innovation was crucial, but it required the temperance of practicality to become a sustainable and transformative force.

This historical example underscores the delicate balance between innovation and recklessness. While Benz's innovation was technically impressive, it was Ford's practical approach that truly changed the world. It's a testament to the idea that innovation, to be truly transformative, requires more than just bold ideas; it demands prudent execution and consideration of the broader societal impact.

The tension between innovation and recklessness extends far beyond the automotive industry. It is a fundamental question that confronts us in every field, from biotechnology to artificial intelligence, from space exploration to environmental conservation. Each new technological frontier brings with it the potential for profound change, but it also carries the risk of unintended consequences.

In the realm of biotechnology, for instance, the development of gene-editing technologies like CRISPR-Cas9 holds the promise of curing genetic diseases. However, the reckless use of such tools, without ethical considerations and adequate safety precautions, could lead to unforeseen and irreversible genetic consequences.

Similarly, artificial intelligence presents both incredible opportunities and substantial risks. The innovation of AI systems capable of autonomous decision-making can revolutionize industries and improve lives. However, the recklessness of deploying AI without transparency, accountability, and safeguards against bias can result in unintended discrimination and harm.

The exploration of space is another arena where innovation and recklessness walk hand in hand. The audacity to reach for the stars and explore distant planets is inspiring, but the heedless pursuit of space endeavors without careful consideration of the ecological impact and ethical implications can have dire consequences.

Environmental innovation, driven by the urgency of climate change, is yet another arena where the balance between progress and prudence is critical. Developing renewable energy sources and sustainable technologies is essential for our planet's future. However, a reckless disregard for ecological limits and overzealous exploitation of resources can exacerbate environmental crises.

To navigate the treacherous waters between innovation and recklessness, we must cultivate a culture of responsible innovation. This begins with recognizing that innovation does not exist in a vacuum; it is embedded in a complex web of societal, ethical, and environmental considerations. Responsible innovation requires us to think not only about what we can achieve but also about how we achieve it.

Ethical considerations are paramount. Innovation must be guided by a moral compass that prioritizes human rights, equality, and justice. This means avoiding technologies or practices that could lead to discrimination, exploitation, or harm. It means addressing the ethical implications of our innovations proactively rather than reactively.

Sustainability is another crucial aspect of responsible innovation. We must consider the long-term consequences of our actions and innovations on the planet. This requires a commitment to reducing environmental impact, conserving resources, and minimizing waste. Sustainable innovation aims to create a harmonious relationship between human progress and the natural world.

Transparency and accountability are essential elements of responsible innovation. Openly sharing information about the development and deployment of new technologies allows for public scrutiny and input. Accountability ensures that those responsible for innovations are held responsible for any negative consequences that may arise.

Education and awareness play a vital role in responsible innovation. Society must be informed about the potential risks and benefits of new technologies, enabling informed decision-making and ethical choices. A well-informed public can also hold innovators and organizations accountable for their actions.

Regulation and governance are tools that can help strike a balance between innovation and recklessness. Governments and international bodies have a role to play in setting standards, enforcing regulations, and ensuring that innovation serves the common good rather than a select few.

Collaboration is another key facet of responsible innovation. Innovators, researchers, policymakers, and civil society must work together to ensure that progress is made responsibly and inclusively. Collaborative approaches can help identify potential pitfalls, mitigate risks, and maximize the positive impact of innovation.

In conclusion, the dance between innovation and recklessness is a nuanced and complex one. While innovation propels us forward and offers the promise of a brighter future, recklessness can lead us astray, causing harm and unintended consequences. Responsible innovation requires us to balance audacity with prudence, to consider not only what we can achieve but also how we achieve it. By fostering a culture of responsible innovation guided by ethical principles, sustainability, transparency, and collaboration, we can harness the power of progress while minimizing the risks of recklessness. In doing so, we can ensure that our innovations truly benefit humanity and the world we inhabit.

CHAPTER EIGHTEEN

Identity's Waters: Patriotism versus Nationalism

Patriotism and nationalism are two concepts that have long stirred the sentiments of individuals, nations, and even civilizations. Both convey a deep attachment and love for one's homeland, yet their manifestations and consequences differ dramatically. To understand this distinction, one must delve into the nuances that lie beneath the surface.

Patriotism, often regarded as the nobler of the two, embodies a love for one's country that is rooted in a genuine appreciation for its virtues, values, and potential for progress. It's akin to a seasoned captain steering a ship with steady hands through the often turbulent waters of national identity. A patriot takes pride in their nation's accomplishments, celebrates its cultural diversity, and aspires to contribute positively to its growth. In essence, patriotism is not merely an expression of attachment to one's country; it is a commitment to nurturing and uplifting it, recognizing that unity and collaboration with the wider world are vital components of progress.

Conversely, nationalism, despite sharing a similar terrain with patriotism, navigates these waters with a different compass. It tends to raise the flag not as a symbol of hope and unity but as a declaration of superiority. Nationalism can be likened to a captain who hoists the flag not as an invitation for collaboration but as a means of asserting dominance. It often espouses an exclusionary approach, delineating who belongs and who does not, leading to the creation of boundaries, both physical and psychological. This exclusivity can manifest in intolerance toward other cultures, a mistrust of outsiders, and a propensity for isolationism.

The paradox between patriotism and nationalism becomes apparent when we scrutinize the essence of these ideologies. True patriotism is rooted in a deep love for one's country but does not necessitate hostility or aggression towards others. It is the understanding that a nation is a mosaic of cultures, ideas, and backgrounds, each contributing to its richness. Patriotism respects diversity, acknowledging that the collective strength of a nation arises from the harmonious coexistence of its varied constituents. In this sense, patriotism does not seek to undermine the value of other nations or peoples but rather fosters an ethos of cooperation, recognizing the interdependence of countries in our globalized era.

In contrast, nationalism, although it may carry the same banner, tends to obscure this broader perspective. It often champions a singular view: the supremacy of one's own nation over all others. This myopic worldview can lead to suspicion and hostility toward other nations, effectively barricading a nation from the potential benefits of international cooperation. Nationalism can breed an "us versus them" mentality that, historically, has contributed to the eruption of conflicts and wars. The danger lies in the assumption that elevating one's nation to the detriment of others is not only justifiable but laudable.

To further illustrate this distinction, one might consider the implications of each ideology on a global scale. A patriot, appreciating their own nation's unique strengths, sees the potential for mutual benefit in engaging with other countries. They understand that in the interconnected world of today, nations rise or fall together, and cooperation is often more conducive to prosperity than isolationism.

In contrast, a nationalist, driven by the pursuit of supremacy, might inadvertently steer their nation into turbulent waters. The focus on dominance, while initially enticing, can lead to diplomatic tensions, trade disputes, and, in extreme cases, conflict. The idea of "America First," for example, is a form of nationalism that prioritizes the interests of the United States above all else. While this approach may appeal to some, it can strain international relations and hinder global cooperation on critical issues like climate change, health pandemics, or economic stability.

Moreover, nationalism can give rise to xenophobia and ethnocentrism, where individuals within a nation begin to view outsiders with suspicion or disdain. This not only erodes the fabric of multicultural societies but also hampers the free flow of ideas and innovation that often arises from cultural exchange and collaboration.

It is essential to note that the boundaries between patriotism and nationalism are not always distinct. In practice, individuals and movements may intertwine elements of both, making it challenging to categorize ideologies neatly. However, the critical distinction lies in their primary focus and consequences. Patriotism, as we have defined it, emphasizes love for one's country while embracing the broader world and fostering cooperation. Nationalism, by contrast, often leans towards an exclusionary, supremacy-oriented approach that can lead to division, mistrust, and conflict.

In conclusion, the contrast between patriotism and nationalism is not merely an academic exercise; it has real-world implications for the way nations interact, cooperate, or clash. The dynamics of these ideologies are continually evolving, shaped by historical events, political movements, and individual perspectives. Therefore, it is imperative for individuals, communities, and societies to engage in thoughtful reflection on the implications of these ideologies and consider how they align with the values of unity, cooperation, and mutual respect in an interconnected world.

CHAPTER NINETEEN

Perception's Prism: Wisdom in the Face of Cynicism

In the grand narrative of human existence, two contrasting philosophies, wisdom and cynicism, emerge as significant players, each wielding its unique influence on how we perceive and engage with the world. These philosophical standpoints, like divergent lenses, color our perspectives and drive our actions, embodying the eternal tug-of-war between optimism and skepticism, trust and doubt, illumination and shadow.

Wisdom, often portrayed as the sagacious sage, serves as a beacon guiding us through life's labyrinth. It is the voice of reason that urges us to seek understanding, to mine the treasures buried within the ore of experience, and to revel in the intricate beauty of nuanced thinking. Wisdom whispers in our ears that even in the darkest of storms, a silver lining may be found, that adversity is a crucible from which resilience emerges, and that the bridges of empathy and compassion can span the widest of chasms.

Yet, wisdom's path is not without its treacherous pitfalls. In its pursuit of profound comprehension, it can occasionally stumble into the realm of naivety. It tends to paint an excessively optimistic picture, blurring the harsher contours of reality. Wisdom may incline us to trust unreservedly, even when caution should be exercised, or to search for meaning in situations where none may exist.

On the contrary, cynicism, often personified as the astute skeptic, is the sentinel that guards the gates of our trust and the bastion against deception and hollow promises. It demands that we see the world through a lens that unveils its true, unvarnished nature. Cynicism is the champion of critical thinking, the voice that challenges the status quo, often unveiling uncomfortable truths that wisdom might conveniently gloss over.

However, cynicism is no less complex. Its relentless doubt and distrust can breed isolation, corroding the very bonds of trust and goodwill that hold societies together. It can stifle innovation and hope, trapping us in a cycle of negativity where solutions appear futile and optimism becomes a distant, fading memory.

The paradox lies in the realization that wisdom and cynicism are not binary opposites, eternally good or bad, but rather instruments—tools that can be wielded, balanced, and refined. Wisdom thrives when we imbibe the lessons of our past and nurture the garden of empathy, tempered by a judicious dose of skepticism. Cynicism serves us well when it prompts us to question, to scrutinize, to discern, but it must coexist with an openness to solutions and an acceptance of the potential for positive change.

The interplay of wisdom and cynicism forms the complex tapestry of human cognition and behavior. It is the pivot upon which our understanding of the world turns, and the fulcrum of our moral and ethical compass. To navigate this delicate dance requires discernment in our judgments, compassion in our interactions, and a willingness to traverse the myriad shades of gray that constitute our multifaceted world.

True wisdom, then, perhaps lies not in choosing one side over the other, but in mastering the art of perception—an art that recognizes the rich complexity in the interplay of these dualities, an art that celebrates the kaleidoscope of human existence where the wisdom of discernment and the vigilance of cynicism coexist harmoniously. It is in this coexistence that we find the keys to unlocking the deepest mysteries of the human condition, and in the recognition of their symbiotic relationship, we discover the true essence of perception itself.

Each perspective, wisdom and cynicism, contributes its unique color to the canvas of our lives, adding depth and dimension to our understanding. The path to enlightenment lies not in shunning one for the other, but in embracing both as integral facets of the human experience.

Wisdom, as the ever-curious sage, encourages us to learn from our past, to savor the richness of life's many flavors, and to relish the splendor of diversity. It beckons us to seek meaning in the symphony of existence, reminding us that even in the most profound of complexities, patterns and purpose may yet emerge.

Cynicism, the vigilant sentinel, reminds us that healthy skepticism is the guardian of truth and transparency. It serves as a necessary counterbalance, a reminder that not all that glitters is gold, and that discernment is a vital tool in navigating the labyrinth of life.

Yet, within this intricate interplay of wisdom and cynicism, we find room for growth and transformation. Wisdom can evolve into a wellspring of genuine insight when coupled with a cautious and discerning eye. Cynicism, when harnessed constructively, can spark change and innovation by pushing the boundaries of the known.

Moreover, it is essential to recognize that these perspectives are not static but dynamic; they are tools that we can hone and adjust according to context. The ability to discern when to lean into wisdom's embrace and when to invoke the scrutiny of cynicism is a hallmark of intellectual and emotional maturity.

Consider the example of a business leader. Wisdom may guide them to appreciate the value of team collaboration, while cynicism can serve as a guard against blind trust in potential partners or ventures. The synergy between these perspectives can lead to well-informed decisions and meaningful progress.

In matters of governance, wisdom can inform leaders to prioritize the welfare of their constituents, while a measured degree of cynicism can prevent them from falling victim to corruption or manipulation. The art of governance, then, becomes a delicate balancing act where these dualities converge.

In personal relationships, wisdom encourages empathy and understanding, fostering deeper connections. Cynicism, when judiciously applied, can protect individuals from emotional harm, ensuring that trust is earned rather than bestowed recklessly. The synergy between these perspectives forms the basis of healthy and fulfilling connections.

In conclusion, the dichotomy of wisdom and cynicism is not a stark either-or proposition but a nuanced and dynamic interplay. To harness the full potential of these perspectives is to embrace the intricate beauty of the human experience, where shades of gray prevail, and the pursuit of truth and growth is a continuous, evolving journey.

As we navigate the multifaceted world that surrounds us, may we find inspiration in the delicate dance of wisdom and cynicism. Let us cultivate the art of perception, recognizing that both perspectives enrich our understanding and contribute to the vibrant mosaic of human existence.

So, in the grand tapestry of life, let us celebrate the wisdom that guides us and the discerning skepticism that protects us. For it is in this harmonious coexistence that we unlock the secrets of our shared journey—a journey where perception becomes an art form, and the human spirit soars to ever-greater heights.

CHAPTER TWENTY

Compassion's Canvas: Navigating Kindness and Naivety

In the intricate tapestry of human emotions and behaviors, the dual concepts of kindness and naivety represent a fascinating, yet often perplexing, interplay of values and perceptions. These two facets of human nature embody the complexities of compassion, benevolence, and trust. They share common ground in their outward expression of goodwill, but beneath the surface, they diverge significantly in their understanding of the world and the potential consequences of their actions.

At its core, kindness is a virtue celebrated across cultures and societies as a beacon of human goodness. It reflects an individual's capacity to empathize with others, to extend a helping hand, and to contribute positively to the well-being of those in need. Kindness resonates with an innate understanding that in a world riddled with challenges and hardships, a simple act of compassion can illuminate the darkest corners of the human experience. It embodies the idea that, fundamentally, people are deserving of benevolence and deserve to be treated with dignity and respect.

Yet, within the realm of compassion, there lies an intriguing paradox—an intersection with naivety, a concept that can be seen as both the shadow and foil of kindness. Naivety, in its purest form, represents a profound trust in the inherent goodness of others. It manifests as an unwavering belief in the sincerity of words and actions, an optimism that often overlooks the potential for deceit or manipulation. It is the manifestation of an untarnished idealism that remains untouched by the cynicism that life's trials and tribulations can sometimes bring.

To comprehend the nuances of this dichotomy, we must explore how kindness and naivety manifest themselves in various facets of human interactions. The acts of kindness we encounter daily, whether they be a simple smile, a charitable gesture, or an empathetic response to someone's suffering, all emanate from a place of genuine concern and empathy. They represent the beauty of human connection—a willingness to extend warmth, care, and understanding to others.

However, it is in the subtleties and complexities of human interaction that the distinction between kindness and naivety becomes more pronounced. Kindness is a virtue that thrives when coupled with discernment and a nuanced understanding of the intricacies of human nature. It recognizes the importance of balance, understanding that while many may reciprocate acts of kindness, others may take advantage of such goodwill. This recognition underscores the need for boundaries and a keen awareness of potential exploitation.

Naivety, on the other hand, often operates in a realm of unguarded trust. It might fail to perceive the subtle cues that suggest ulterior motives or the hidden agendas of others. Naive individuals, driven by their unwavering faith in the goodness of humanity, may inadvertently place themselves or others in situations where manipulation or exploitation becomes a possibility.

In essence, kindness, when informed by wisdom and experience, is the embodiment of a compassionate discernment—an understanding that while the intention may be to extend goodwill, there is a need to exercise judgment in discerning when, where, and how that goodwill should be shared. It acknowledges the existence of those who may not reciprocate kindness with gratitude but still recognizes the value in extending empathy and support.

Conversely, naivety, though well-intentioned, operates in a state of vulnerability. It is an innocence that may be taken advantage of, as it tends to overlook the complexities and sometimes darker shades of human behavior. While its idealism is admirable, it may expose individuals to risks and exploitation, and it can lead to disillusionment when confronted with the harsh realities of the world.

A key aspect of the contrast between kindness and naivety is their relationship with trust. Kindness operates on the premise that trust can be extended but may need to be earned, while naivety operates on the premise that trust should be given unconditionally. The former recognizes that trust is a valuable commodity, one that should be carefully dispensed based on mutual respect and understanding. The latter, driven by a belief in the innate goodness of humanity, extends trust without reservations, often without consideration for potential consequences.

Kindness, in its most profound form, is an act of conscious choice—a deliberate decision to bring light and positivity into the world, even when faced with adversity. It embodies the wisdom to navigate the delicate balance between empathy and self-preservation, understanding that while the desire to help others is noble, it should not come at the cost of one's own well-being.

In contrast, naivety may stem from a lack of experience, a sheltered upbringing, or an idealistic worldview. It often thrives in environments where individuals have not been exposed to the darker aspects of human behavior. It represents an innocence that may persist until it encounters situations that challenge its core beliefs.

The consequences of naivety can be profound. Individuals who exhibit an excessive degree of naivety may find themselves vulnerable to manipulation, deceit, and exploitation. They may struggle to recognize when others are acting with less-than-honorable intentions, leading to potential harm, both emotionally and materially.

The interplay between kindness and naivety is not confined to individual interactions alone; it also permeates societal structures and policies. In the context of larger social dynamics, kindness often aligns with efforts to create a more equitable and compassionate society. It drives initiatives aimed at alleviating suffering, promoting justice, and championing the rights of marginalized communities.

However, the impact of kindness can be amplified or hindered by the presence of naivety within society. When naivety prevails at the societal level, it can lead to misplaced trust in institutions or leaders that may not have the best interests of the population at heart. It can hinder efforts to address systemic issues and may perpetuate injustices under the guise of goodwill.

The delicate balance between kindness and naivety is a theme that resonates in various realms of literature, art, and culture. In literature, characters who embody these traits often serve as mirrors to the complexities of human nature. The naive character may symbolize innocence and purity, while the kind character represents the capacity for empathy and altruism. These characters' journeys often explore the transformation and growth that occur as they navigate the challenges and conflicts arising from their respective dispositions.

Artistic interpretations of kindness and naivety can offer viewers a unique perspective on these qualities. Paintings, films, and other forms of artistic expression can capture the beauty of kindness and the vulnerability of naivety. They can evoke empathy and provoke contemplation on the implications of trust and goodwill in a world where motivations are not always transparent.

The exploration of kindness and naivety extends beyond the realms of psychology, philosophy, and literature; it has practical implications in various aspects of life. In education, for instance, educators may grapple with striking a balance between fostering a sense of trust and idealism in their students while also equipping them with critical thinking skills to navigate the complexities of the world. Similarly, leaders and policymakers must consider the role of trust and discernment in their decision-making processes, especially when dealing with issues of public welfare and justice.

It is essential to recognize that the interplay between kindness and naivety is not a static binary but exists on a spectrum. People may exhibit varying degrees of each quality, and these qualities may evolve over time as individuals gain experience and wisdom. An individual who once embodied unbridled naivety may, with the passage of time and life's lessons, cultivate a deeper sense of kindness tempered by discernment.

In conclusion, the exploration of kindness and naivety is a profound journey into the complexities of human nature and human interaction. Both qualities celebrate the innate goodness of humanity, yet they differ significantly in their understanding of trust, discernment, and the potential consequences of their actions.

Kindness, when informed by wisdom and experience, represents a deliberate choice to extend compassion and empathy while exercising discernment. It embodies the belief that, in a world filled with contrasts and contradictions, the genuine desire to help others should not be overshadowed by a lack of judgment.

Conversely, naivety is an innocence that often exists in a state of vulnerability. It represents a belief in the purity of human intentions but may overlook the darker shades of human behavior. While admirable in its idealism, naivety may expose individuals to risks and exploitation.

The key to navigating this intricate spectrum lies in finding the balance between kindness and discernment. It is an acknowledgment that, while compassion is a virtue to be celebrated, trust should be dispensed with care and consideration. It is an invitation to engage in a lifelong journey of self-awareness and growth—a journey where the dance between kindness and naivety continues, shaped by the wisdom of experience and the desire to make the world a better place.

CHAPTER TWENTY-ONE

Vanity's Veil: Balancing Health and Vanity

In the intricate tapestry of human existence, one of the most fascinating and perpetual struggles is the tension between health and vanity. These two aspects of our lives represent contrasting facets of our desires, values, and priorities. They often exist in a delicate equilibrium, yet this balance can be difficult to maintain. To understand this intricate dance, we must delve deep into the realm of human motivations and the complexities of modern society.

At its core, "health" is an intrinsic good—a manifestation of our biological and psychological well-being. Pursuing health entails a commitment to nourishing our bodies with wholesome food, engaging in regular exercise, and safeguarding our mental tranquility. It's a journey toward vitality, longevity, and a heightened quality of life. The quest for health is, undeniably, a noble and virtuous endeavor.

However, the pursuit of health can, at times, take an extreme turn. It transforms from a genuine quest for well-being into an obsession with unattainable standards. This unhealthy manifestation is exemplified by a culture fixated on the perfect physique, where each meal is a calculated equation and physical appearance becomes an unyielding measuring stick. In this dark corner of health, individuals may find themselves ensnared by anxiety, eating disorders, and the relentless pressure to conform to societal notions of beauty.

On the opposite side of this intricate scale, we encounter "vanity"—the realm where aesthetics and personal presentation take precedence. Vanity isn't inherently malevolent; it encompasses the very human desire to present oneself in the best light, to take pleasure in looking and feeling good. When balanced, vanity can be a source of self-confidence and a contributor to positive mental health. It encourages us to groom ourselves, select stylish clothing, and take pride in our appearance.

However, vanity can also take on a darker shade when it becomes an all-encompassing obsession. It's the territory where external appearances overshadow inner substance. It's the pursuit of an idealized, often unattainable image of beauty. In this extreme form, individuals may embark on drastic diets, risky cosmetic procedures, or adhere to unsustainable beauty standards, all at the cost of their holistic well-being and authenticity.

The challenge that confronts us is to discover a harmonious middle ground—a place where health and vanity coexist in symbiotic harmony. Achieving this balance requires us to embrace our bodies' natural beauty, recognizing that our imperfections are an integral part of our uniqueness. Simultaneously, we must prioritize self-care, nurturing our physical and mental well-being, and avoiding the pitfalls of either extreme.

In this pursuit, it's imperative to comprehend that health is not merely defined by the absence of physical blemishes or a particular body shape. True health encompasses vitality, happiness, self-acceptance, and a holistic sense of well-being. Vanity, when harnessed positively, can complement this pursuit by enhancing self-esteem, promoting self-love, and instilling confidence.

The interplay between health and vanity reflects the complexity of the human experience. It beckons us to examine our values, to discern what truly matters, and to strike a balance that enriches our lives without overshadowing our authenticity. This intricate dance invites us to cultivate a healthier and more balanced existence—one where both health and vanity serve as allies on our journey of self-discovery.

To navigate this complex terrain, we must foster a society that champions diversity, celebrates individuality, and encourages self-acceptance. Such a society would acknowledge that each person's journey towards health and self-expression is unique, recognizing that external appearances are but one facet of a multidimensional being.

In the realm of health, the emphasis should shift from mere aesthetics to holistic well-being. Instead of aspiring to conform to unrealistic beauty ideals, we should celebrate and support one another's efforts to maintain healthy lifestyles, focusing on inner and outer vitality, free from judgment.

Moreover, we must instill in ourselves and future generations the importance of self-acceptance and self-love. This can be achieved by nurturing emotional intelligence, resilience, and mental health. By teaching individuals to value themselves beyond external attributes, we foster a culture of self-assuredness that transcends the fleeting allure of vanity.

Simultaneously, in the world of vanity, there is room for introspection. We should critically examine the unrealistic beauty standards perpetuated by media and society, recognizing that they often lead to harmful practices and toxic comparisons. Instead, we can champion a more inclusive definition of beauty, one that appreciates diversity in all its forms.

The fashion and beauty industries, as powerful influencers, bear a responsibility to encourage authenticity and diversity. By showcasing models of various sizes, ethnicities, and gender identities, they can redefine the very notion of beauty and inspire confidence in individuals who may otherwise feel marginalized.

Furthermore, it's crucial to foster open conversations about the realities of both health and vanity. By dispelling myths and dispelling stigmas, we empower individuals to make informed choices and seek help when needed. A culture that normalizes discussions about mental health, body image, and self-esteem can provide essential support to those navigating the complex terrain of health and beauty.

In educational institutions, curricula should emphasize the importance of holistic well-being, teaching students not only about physical health but also about mental health, emotional intelligence, and the value of authenticity. Education can be a powerful tool in nurturing future generations who prioritize self-acceptance and self-care.

Moreover, it's incumbent upon us as individuals to reflect upon our own attitudes toward health and vanity. We can embark on journeys of self-discovery, engaging in practices that promote self-compassion and self-awareness. By doing so, we become more resilient against societal pressures and more capable of achieving a balanced perspective.

As we navigate this intricate interplay between health and vanity, we must remember that these are but two facets of our multifaceted lives. Both are essential aspects of the human experience, and both have the potential to enrich our journey of self-discovery.

In the end, the balance between health and vanity is not a static point but a dynamic process. It requires continuous self-reflection, adaptation, and self-love. It calls for a society that celebrates authenticity and diversity, a culture that promotes holistic well-being, and individuals who embrace their uniqueness.

When we achieve this balance, we embark on a journey of self-acceptance, self-love, and true well-being. We become champions of our own authenticity, and we inspire others to do the same. In this harmonious coexistence of health and vanity, we discover not only our outer beauty but, more importantly, the beauty of our inner selves—the essence of what makes us uniquely human.

CHAPTER TWENTY-TWO

Harmony Found: The Delicate Balance of Peace and Appeasement

In the intricate world of international diplomacy and conflict resolution, the dichotomy between peace and appeasement is a theme that has consistently shaped the course of history. While these two concepts seem to exist at opposing ends of the political spectrum, where peace symbolizes harmony, cooperation, and conflict resolution, and appeasement carries connotations of compromise and capitulation, the reality is far more nuanced. This nuanced exploration reveals that peace and appeasement often coexist in a complex and delicate balance, each with its own merits and pitfalls.

At its core, peace represents an aspirational ideal. It encapsulates humanity's collective desire for global harmony, where nations coexist without resorting to violence or armed conflict. The pursuit of peace is inherently noble, driven by the desire to create a world where diplomacy prevails over destruction, where lives are protected, and where cooperation thrives.

The path to peace is often characterized by diplomacy, dialogue, and compromise. Nations and leaders strive to find common ground, seek peaceful resolutions to disputes, and avoid the devastating consequences of war. In this context, peace becomes a beacon of hope, illuminating the possibility of a world where nations resolve their differences through discourse rather than force.

Conversely, appeasement is often perceived as a flawed strategy in international relations. It entails making concessions or compromises to an aggressor in the hope of avoiding conflict or achieving temporary peace. Critics argue that appeasement can undermine a nation's principles and values, potentially emboldening aggressors and paving the way for further demands.

However, it is essential to acknowledge that appeasement is not inherently malevolent. At times, it may be a strategic maneuver with the noblest of intentions. Leaders may choose to appease to buy time for diplomacy, protect innocent lives, or prevent a devastating war. In such cases, appeasement is not a sign of moral decay but rather a calculated attempt to avert catastrophe.

To further understand the nuances of appeasement, it is crucial to recognize that it can take various forms. It can be a tactical maneuver aimed at preserving peace temporarily, an acknowledgment of geopolitical realities, or even a pragmatic approach to prevent unnecessary conflict escalation.

The line between peace and appeasement is often a thin one. Deciphering when appeasement transitions from a prudent strategy to a detrimental surrender of principles is a complex task. It requires astute judgment and a deep understanding of the specific geopolitical context.

Ironically, the pursuit of peace, when approached with unyielding rigidity and a refusal to address legitimate concerns, can lead to a superficial tranquility that conceals deep-seated issues. In such cases, peace may merely serve as a facade that masks unresolved conflicts and injustices.

This raises an essential point: true and lasting peace must be built on justice, fairness, and respect for all parties involved. An unwillingness to confront injustices can render peace an empty promise, perpetuating underlying tensions and discontent.

The delicate balance between peace and appeasement presents a moral dilemma. Leaders and nations must grapple with the question of what price they are willing to pay for peace. Is the avoidance of immediate conflict worth compromising on principles and values?

Justice plays a pivotal role in distinguishing between genuine peace and a flawed semblance of it. True peace is not merely the absence of conflict but the presence of fairness and equity. To achieve such a state, addressing historical grievances and rectifying injustices may be necessary.

Examining historical instances can shed light on the complexities of the peace vs. appeasement dilemma. The Treaty of Versailles following World War I, for instance, is often criticized for its punitive nature, contributing to long-term instability and leading to World War II. This historical lesson underscores the importance of pursuing peace through just and equitable means.

Geopolitical realities further complicate the dynamics of peace and appeasement. In a world where power dynamics are in constant flux, nations must navigate a complex web of alliances, rivalries, and interests. The pursuit of peace often involves balancing these factors with the goal of preventing conflicts.

Diplomacy emerges as a critical instrument in the pursuit of peace. Skilled diplomats and negotiators work tirelessly to find common ground, negotiate treaties, and defuse tensions. Diplomatic efforts can be seen as a proactive approach to preventing conflicts, minimizing the need for appeasement.

The ethical dimensions of peace and appeasement also warrant examination. Ethical leaders and nations aspire to maintain their principles while seeking peaceful resolutions. This entails the arduous task of negotiating while upholding a moral compass that guides actions in the international arena.

The peace vs. appeasement debate remains highly relevant in contemporary geopolitics. Recent examples, such as negotiations with North Korea or the Iran nuclear deal, exemplify the challenges and nuances involved in pursuing peaceful solutions while avoiding appeasement.

International organizations, such as the United Nations, are instrumental in facilitating diplomacy and promoting peaceful resolutions. They serve as platforms for dialogue, enabling nations to address conflicts on a global stage and find diplomatic alternatives to appeasement.

A compelling aspect of the peace vs. appeasement discourse is the humanitarian imperative. Protecting innocent lives and preventing widespread suffering often drives nations to consider appeasement as a temporary measure. This humanitarian dimension adds complexity to the ethical calculus.

Conversely, history has also demonstrated that intransigence and the refusal to engage in diplomacy can exact a heavy toll. Stubbornness can lead to prolonged conflicts with devastating consequences, emphasizing the importance of finding a balance between principles and pragmatism.

As we contemplate the dual nature of the peace vs. appeasement duality, it is evident that this is an ongoing and evolving conversation. The evolving nature of geopolitics, the shifting sands of power, and the changing global landscape ensure that this debate remains central to international relations.

In conclusion, the pursuit of peace is an inherently imperfect endeavor. It requires navigating a complex and often treacherous terrain where principles, pragmatism, and moral imperatives intersect. While appeasement is fraught with pitfalls, it can, at times, serve as a pragmatic means to safeguard lives and buy time for diplomatic resolutions. The delicate balance between these two concepts underscores the intricate nature of global politics and the profound challenges involved in achieving a peaceful world. It is a balance that continues to shape the course of history and challenge the ethical compass of nations and leaders alike.

CHAPTER TWENTY-THREE

Knowledge's Odyssey: Education versus Indoctrination

In the vast tapestry of human understanding, few threads are as fundamental as the concepts of education and indoctrination. These two entities, although ostensibly aligned in their pursuit of transmitting knowledge and shaping minds, are separated by a profound moral and philosophical chasm. At first glance, it may appear that education, driven by the noble ambition of enlightening minds, is inherently virtuous, while indoctrination, often perceived as a means to instill a particular set of beliefs or values, is inherently flawed. However, delving deeper into this dichotomy reveals a more nuanced reality.

Education, in its purest form, embodies the principles of enlightenment. It champions the diversity of thought, encourages individuals to question, analyze, and expand their intellectual horizons. True education empowers students to become autonomous thinkers, arming them with a diverse spectrum of knowledge that nurtures critical thinking, empathy, and intellectual curiosity.

A well-rounded education serves as a bridge between ignorance and wisdom, offering students the tools to navigate an increasingly complex world. It is a journey of exploration, where the seeker is encouraged to scrutinize information, seek different perspectives, and formulate their own informed opinions.

However, it is vital to acknowledge that education is not always a flawless beacon of enlightenment. It can harbor imperfections in the form of inadequate teaching methods, biased curricula, or a lack of inclusivity. In such cases, education may inadvertently deter students from embracing its full potential, rendering knowledge inaccessible or irrelevant.

In contrast, indoctrination presents a formidable adversary, masquerading as a benevolent force with an ostensibly noble agenda. Often, it seeks to instill specific values, beliefs, or ideologies in individuals. In some instances, this may be motivated by a genuine desire to uphold a perceived moral high ground or to preserve cultural or societal norms.

The allure of indoctrination lies in its ability to rally individuals around a common cause. It may promise clarity in a complex world and provide a sense of belonging to a community that shares the same convictions. At times, it appeals to the greater good, promising to shape a better future for all.

Yet, beneath the surface, indoctrination conceals a treacherous undercurrent. It has the potential to mold minds into a singular image, stifling dissent and discouraging independent thought. Rather than nurturing critical thinking, indoctrination often promotes unquestioning adherence to a prescribed set of beliefs.

History has borne witness to the darker manifestations of indoctrination, where well-intentioned agendas have led to atrocities. Totalitarian regimes have exploited the power of indoctrination to manipulate entire populations, suppressing dissent and stifling intellectual diversity in the name of a purportedly noble cause.

The education-indoctrination spectrum is not a simple binary, where education is inherently good and indoctrination is inherently bad. Rather, it is a complex continuum where the purity of intent and the methods employed play pivotal roles in determining the ethical standing of a given approach.

Even within education, there exist shades of grey. Educational systems can be influenced by political, cultural, or societal biases that shape curricula and teaching methodologies. These biases may inadvertently propagate inequalities, hinder critical thinking, or reinforce stereotypes.

Conversely, within the realm of indoctrination, noble intentions can often be found. Movements aimed at social justice, environmental conservation, or humanitarian causes may seek to indoctrinate individuals with values that, on the surface, align with the greater good.

The challenge lies in balancing noble intentions with ethical approaches. Even when motivated by a genuine desire to create positive change, indoctrination can become a means to silence dissent and suppress alternative viewpoints.

In light of these complexities, individuals must develop a critical lens through which to evaluate educational and indoctrinational experiences. Critical evaluation involves questioning the sources of knowledge, recognizing bias, and seeking diverse perspectives.

Central to this discourse is the importance of preserving the freedom of thought. Education, at its core, should encourage individuals to explore, question, and form their own conclusions. Indoctrination, when unchecked, poses a threat to this fundamental freedom.

Society, as the custodian of knowledge transmission, plays a pivotal role in shaping the education-indoctrination landscape. Policymakers, educators, and institutions bear a profound responsibility to cultivate an environment where education flourishes and indoctrination is scrutinized.

In the age of the internet and social media, echo chambers have emerged as breeding grounds for both education and indoctrination. They can reinforce existing beliefs and stifle dissenting voices, perpetuating divisive ideologies.

In the pursuit of enlightenment, inclusivity stands as a guiding principle. Educational systems should strive to be inclusive, embracing diverse voices, perspectives, and experiences. This inclusivity serves as a safeguard against the insidious creep of indoctrination.

Ultimately, individuals themselves bear a significant responsibility in navigating the complex waters of education and indoctrination. They must remain vigilant, continuously examining the sources of their knowledge and the approaches employed to impart it.

The dichotomy between education and indoctrination is an ongoing dialogue, one that evolves with the changing tides of society, technology, and human understanding. To engage in this dialogue is to embark on a journey of intellectual growth and self-discovery.

In conclusion, the distinction between education and indoctrination is not a clear-cut divide but a nuanced interplay of intent, approach, and outcomes. Both can be harnessed for positive or negative ends, depending on the ethical considerations that underpin them.

As we navigate the seas of knowledge, let us remain vigilant. Let us champion the cause of genuine education while scrutinizing the encroachments of indoctrination. In this balance lies the promise of a more enlightened, empathetic, and intellectually diverse world, where the pursuit of knowledge is an unwavering commitment to truth and the betterment of humanity.

CHAPTER TWENTY-FOUR

Unraveling Dependency: Navigating Technology's Grip

In the dynamic intersection of human existence and technological advancement, a thought-provoking paradox emerges—the juxtaposition of technology's boundless potential for good and its latent capacity to breed dependency. This juxtaposition prompts us to consider the profound impact of technology on our lives, revealing a complex interplay between empowerment and entrapment.

Technology, at its core, is a tool—a neutral instrument with the power to revolutionize the way we interact, learn, and grow. It extends our reach, enabling connections that transcend geographical boundaries, and it augments our understanding, granting us access to an unprecedented wealth of information. In this light, technology emerges as a herald of progress, promising to propel humanity toward uncharted horizons.

However, as with any powerful tool, the morality of technology lies not in its essence, but in its application. It is in this application that we encounter the subtle transformation of convenience into compulsion. The same technologies that once promised empowerment can, if left unchecked, ensnare us in a cycle of dependency.

Consider, for instance, the allure of convenience that technology affords. Smart devices streamline our daily routines, algorithms anticipate our preferences, and social media platforms facilitate instant connections with loved ones and acquaintances alike. These conveniences, when appropriately managed, enhance our quality of life. Yet, when unbridled, they can become the gateway to dependency, cultivating a reliance on technology that disrupts our ability to engage with the world on a more fundamental level.On a broader scale, technology's potential for societal advancement is staggering. It is a catalyst for innovation, driving breakthroughs in fields as diverse as medicine, energy, and environmental sustainability. It provides the tools with which we can address some of the most pressing global challenges, from climate change to healthcare accessibility.

Yet, even in the pursuit of noble agendas, there lies the risk of unintended consequences. The relentless march of progress may inadvertently lead to job displacement and economic inequality. The digital revolution, while promising unprecedented connectivity, may also foster a divide between those with access and those without, deepening existing inequalities.

This paradox invites us to tread with caution, to approach technology not with blind enthusiasm, but with an informed and discerning eye. It is a call to recognize the potential for empowerment and the specter of dependency in equal measure. By doing so, we can harness technology as a force for good while guarding against its capacity to diminish our authenticity and agency.

Indeed, the crux of this complex interplay lies in our awareness—our ability to discern when technology augments and when it ensnares, when it empowers and when it eclipses our innate capacities. It requires us to be deliberate and intentional in our use of technology, to wield it as a tool for our betterment rather than allowing it to dictate the contours of our existence.

To master this balance is to hold the key to a future where technology serves our highest ideals without sacrificing our essential humanity. It requires a commitment to remain the architects of our own destiny, to resist the allure of convenience when it threatens to lull us into complacency, and to question the trajectory of progress when it veers into potentially perilous territory.

In this duality, the question is not a binary one of technology's inherent virtue or vice, but rather a nuanced exploration of how we choose to employ its remarkable potential. It is an inquiry that hinges on our capacity to strike a delicate equilibrium, to be discerning users of technology rather than unwitting subjects of its allure.

In this equilibrium, we find the path to a future where technology is not a master to which we bow, but a servant that assists in the realization of our highest aspirations. It is a future where dependency is replaced with empowerment, where convenience is tempered by consciousness, and where progress is guided by the moral compass of humanity.

This journey requires vigilance, a commitment to remain ever-mindful of the dual nature of technology. It necessitates an ongoing dialogue, both within ourselves and within our broader society, about the role that technology should play in shaping our collective future.

Ultimately, the narrative of technology and dependency is a story we are collectively writing. It is a narrative that calls for introspection, for thoughtful consideration of our relationship with the digital realm, and for deliberate choices about how we integrate technology into the tapestry of our lives.

As we navigate this intricate landscape, let us do so with a sense of purpose, with an understanding that our choices today will reverberate through generations to come. Let us approach technology not with trepidation, but with a sense of agency, recognizing that we hold the power to shape its impact on our lives and on the world at large.

In doing so, we embrace the potential for a future where technology and humanity coexist in harmonious synergy, each amplifying the strengths of the other. It is a future where the promise of progress is met with a tempered wisdom, where the conveniences of the digital age enhance rather than supplant our essential human connections.

In this future, technology is not an end in itself, but a means to a greater end—a tool with which we can build a more inclusive, sustainable, and compassionate world. It is a future where the duality of technology and dependency is not a source of conflict, but a wellspring of opportunity and growth.

So, let us embark on this journey of exploration with a sense of purpose and a spirit of inquiry. Let us engage with technology not as passive consumers, but as active participants in the ongoing evolution of our digital age. And let us do so with a vision of a future that embraces the complexities of our relationship with technology, steering it toward a destination that reflects our highest aspirations.

As we navigate this terrain, let us be guided by a fundamental belief—that we, as individuals and as a society, have the capacity to harness the potential of technology for the betterment of all. It is a belief that acknowledges the challenges and uncertainties that lie ahead, but also celebrates the immense promise that technology holds.

In the end, the paradox of technology and dependency is not a puzzle to be solved, but a profound exploration of our own humanity. It is a reminder that, as we stand on the threshold of an increasingly digital age, we must be not only masters of technology but also stewards of our own moral compass.

In this unfolding narrative, the power to shape the future rests firmly in our hands. It is a power we wield not with trepidation, but with the knowledge that, with mindfulness and intention, we can navigate the delicate dance between technology and dependency, forging a path toward a future that embodies the very best of our shared human potential.

CHAPTER TWENTY-FIVE

Life's Contrasts: The Art of Moderation and Deprivation

In the grand tapestry of existence, Moderation and Deprivation stand as two distinct but intertwined threads, each offering its own unique perspective on how we navigate life's offerings. Moderation, with its delicate touch, advocates for a measured approach, urging us to partake in life's pleasures with temperance. It encourages the embrace of variety, acknowledging that indulgence, when tempered, can be a source of enrichment. However, while Moderation carries the banner of balance, it can sometimes tread perilously close to complacency. In its pursuit of equilibrium, Moderation may inadvertently lead to a life half-lived, where the vivid hues of experience are dulled into shades of gray.

Deprivation, on the other hand, embodies a stern resolve to exercise discipline and restraint. It insists on denying certain pleasures in the pursuit of a higher, virtuous purpose. The philosophy of Deprivation is rooted in the belief that by relinquishing excess, we forge a path towards greater well-being. However, this noble pursuit is not without its pitfalls. The stringent measures advocated by Deprivation can breed resentment and unfulfilled desires. It runs the risk of extinguishing the very passions that lend vibrancy to our lives, leaving us in a barren wasteland of unmet aspirations.

Yet, it is within the interplay of these contrasting forces that the true art of living is found. Rather than seeking an absolute allegiance to either side, perhaps the path to a fulfilling life lies in the delicate dance between Moderation and Deprivation. It is a dynamic equilibrium, where Moderation tempers the rigidity of Deprivation, and Deprivation bestows a sense of purpose and direction upon Moderation. This symphonic interplay allows us to navigate life's myriad offerings, finding a rhythm that resonates with our unique composition.

In the pursuit of Moderation, we discover the wisdom of savouring life's pleasures without succumbing to excess. It calls for an understanding that true abundance lies not in accumulating, but in savoring the richness of each experience. However, Moderation, when taken to an extreme, can metamorphose into a form of self-imposed restraint, stifling the very vitality it seeks to protect. It is a fine line that requires constant discernment and calibration.

Conversely, the philosophy of Deprivation brings with it a sense of purpose and discipline. It encourages us to discern between true needs and transient desires, empowering us to navigate life's offerings with a discerning eye. Yet, Deprivation, when untempered by the wisdom of Moderation, runs the risk of becoming an oppressive force, depriving us of the very joys that make life worth living.

The art of harmonizing Moderation and Deprivation is a dynamic process, one that requires constant attunement to the rhythms of our own existence. It is a symphony where the notes of temperance are complemented by the chords of discipline, creating a composition that is uniquely our own. In this delicate dance, we find the true essence of a life well-lived.

At its core, the interplay of Moderation and Deprivation invites us to question our relationship with the world around us. It prompts us to consider not only what we consume, but how we consume it. It challenges us to discern between true fulfillment and momentary gratification, urging us to seek depth over superficiality. It is a call to engage with life's offerings with intentionality and purpose.

In this exploration, it is essential to recognize that the balance between Moderation and Deprivation is not a static state, but a fluid and dynamic equilibrium. It is a process that requires ongoing self-reflection, a willingness to adapt, and a keen awareness of our own evolving needs and desires. It is an art that invites us to be present, to listen to the whispers of our own soul, and to respond with wisdom and discernment.

Ultimately, the pursuit of Moderation and Deprivation is a deeply personal journey, one that is shaped by our own values, aspirations, and experiences. It is a testament to the complexity and richness of the human experience, inviting us to navigate the contours of our own existence with grace and intention. It is a reminder that the art of living lies not in rigid adherence to one philosophy or the other, but in the ability to dance between the contrasting notes of Moderation and Deprivation, creating a symphony that is uniquely our own.

In the grand tapestry of existence, Moderation and Deprivation are not opposing forces, but complementary aspects of a holistic approach to life. They offer us a framework for engaging with the world around us, guiding us towards a deeper understanding of ourselves and our place in the world. Through the delicate interplay of Moderation and Deprivation, we uncover a path towards greater fulfillment, a life that is both rich in experience and purposeful in its pursuits. It is an invitation to embark on a journey of self-discovery, to explore the depths of our own desires and aspirations, and to navigate the complexities of the human experience with wisdom and grace.

CHAPTER TWENTY-SIX

Balance of Being: Conservation versus Hoarding

In the world of possessions and acquisitions, there exists a fine line between conservation and hoarding, and the distinction between the two often lies in intent and approach.

On one side, we find the conservationist, someone driven by the noble aim of preserving resources for the common good. They carefully collect and protect valuable items, recognizing their potential significance for future generations. This approach embodies a sense of responsibility, ensuring that scarce resources are not squandered but utilized wisely. It's an act of stewardship, an acknowledgment of our duty to safeguard the environment and our heritage.

The conservationist's journey begins with a deep appreciation for the treasures of our world. Whether it be rare books, endangered species, or historical artifacts, they understand that these items hold the keys to understanding our past and shaping our future. Theirs is a quest to strike a harmonious balance between enjoying the benefits of these possessions and ensuring they endure for generations to come.

This path leads to sustainability, as the conservationist promotes mindful consumption and the protection of valuable resources. In essence, they act as guardians of the planet's natural and cultural heritage, preserving it not just for their own enjoyment but for the enrichment of humanity as a whole. It is a selfless endeavor, driven by an altruistic agenda focused on the greater good.

On the other side, there's the hoarder, whose actions may seem similar but are guided by an entirely different motive. They accumulate possessions not out of a sense of responsibility but rather from an innate fear of loss. Hoarders amass items indiscriminately, often to excess, believing that the sheer quantity of possessions equates to security. It's a response born of insecurity, a misguided attempt to fill emotional voids with material objects.

The hoarder's journey is one fraught with emotional turmoil. They often struggle with letting go, fearing that any reduction in their collection will leave them vulnerable to life's uncertainties. This attachment to possessions can become suffocating, isolating them from meaningful relationships and experiences. The excessive accumulation often obscures the truly valuable items and can hinder personal growth. The good agenda of safeguarding one's assets becomes overshadowed by the compulsion to acquire more, losing sight of the initial intention.

Ultimately, the difference between these two perspectives lies not only in the physical possessions but in the underlying motivations. Conservation is an act of mindful stewardship, while hoarding is driven by fear and attachment. Recognizing this distinction allows us to navigate the path toward responsible resource management, embracing conservation while avoiding the pitfalls of hoarding.

In essence, the conservationist's approach represents a measured and deliberate response to the challenges of a world with finite resources. They advocate for thoughtful consumption, recycling, and the responsible use of energy. Their commitment to conservation extends beyond material possessions; it includes protecting the environment, advocating for sustainable practices, and cherishing the wisdom passed down through generations.

It prompts us to reflect on our own actions and intentions, encouraging a more thoughtful and sustainable approach to the possessions we hold dear. We must ask ourselves whether our acquisitions are driven by genuine need or by a deeper psychological desire for security through material wealth. By doing so, we can avoid falling into the trap of hoarding and instead become conscious stewards of our possessions.

In a world where consumerism often runs rampant, the conservationist's perspective is a refreshing reminder that less can indeed be more. It encourages us to value quality over quantity, experiences over possessions, and the well-being of our planet over the relentless pursuit of more things.

Conservationists serve as beacons of hope, reminding us that we can lead fulfilling lives without drowning in material excess. They inspire us to reevaluate our priorities and recognize that the true measure of wealth lies not in what we own but in the positive impact we can have on the world around us.

In conclusion, the delicate balance between conservation and hoarding is a reflection of our inner values and intentions. It is a choice between contributing to a sustainable future or succumbing to the insecurities of the present. The conservationist's path offers a blueprint for responsible resource management, urging us to tread lightly on this Earth and leave a legacy of wisdom, beauty, and abundance for generations to come.

The conservationist's approach extends beyond material possessions; it encompasses a deep respect for nature and its intricate ecosystems. Those who champion conservation understand that the delicate balance of the natural world is as important as safeguarding human-made treasures. They advocate for the preservation of biodiversity, realizing that every species plays a unique role in maintaining the health of our planet.

Moreover, conservationists often engage in educational efforts, sharing their knowledge and passion with others. They recognize that by imparting wisdom about responsible resource management and the importance of preservation, they can inspire future generations to follow in their footsteps. This educational aspect of conservation extends the impact far beyond the individual.

In contrast, hoarding often leads to isolation. Hoarders may find themselves surrounded by possessions, but these material riches do not fill the emotional void within. The fear of losing these possessions becomes all-consuming, driving a wedge between them and the outside world. Friends and family may struggle to understand the hoarder's compulsive behavior, further deepening their isolation.

For the conservationist, the joy comes not from the act of acquisition itself but from the knowledge that they are contributing to a greater purpose. It's a purpose that extends beyond their own lifetime, creating a legacy of responsible stewardship for future generations. This perspective provides a deep sense of fulfillment and purpose, contributing to mental and emotional well-being.

One of the key distinctions between conservation and hoarding is the notion of responsibility. Conservationists embrace their responsibility to society and the planet. They understand that by preserving and protecting valuable resources, they are contributing to a more sustainable and equitable world. This sense of responsibility extends to advocating for policies and practices that promote conservation on a larger scale.

On the other hand, hoarders often shirk their responsibilities, as their compulsive accumulation can lead to neglect of other essential aspects of life. Financial stability, relationships, and personal well-being may all suffer as a result of their hoarding behavior. The initial intention to safeguard possessions becomes overshadowed by the chaos and disarray that often accompany hoarding.

The conservationist's journey is one of enlightenment. They continuously seek to expand their knowledge about the objects, species, or ecosystems they are passionate about preserving. This quest for understanding adds depth to their appreciation and allows them to make informed decisions about how best to protect what they hold dear.

In contrast, hoarders may accumulate items without fully understanding their value or significance. The emotional attachment to possessions can cloud their judgment, making it difficult for them to discern between what is genuinely valuable and what is merely clutter. This lack of discernment can lead to overwhelming and chaotic living environments.

Conservationists often form communities of like-minded individuals who share their passion for preserving the world's treasures. These communities provide support, encouragement, and a sense of belonging. They understand that the journey of conservation can be challenging at times and that having a network of fellow conservationists can make a significant difference.

Hoarders, on the other hand, may find it challenging to connect with others who understand their compulsion. Their behavior can be isolating, leading to a sense of shame and secrecy. Breaking free from the cycle of hoarding often requires professional intervention and support, as the hoarder may not have the tools or resources to address their issues on their own.

In the grand tapestry of life, the conservationist's role is that of a caretaker, tending to the

threads that weave together the story of our planet. They recognize that every action they take, no matter how small, can have a ripple effect on the world around them. This awareness drives them to make choices that are not only sustainable but also considerate of the interconnectedness of all living things.

In contrast, hoarders may unintentionally harm the environment by hoarding items that could be recycled or repurposed. Their excessive consumption can contribute to resource depletion and environmental degradation, further highlighting the difference in impact between the two approaches.

The conservationist's mindset extends to the larger global community. They understand that in an increasingly interconnected world, conservation is a shared responsibility. Climate change, habitat loss, and the extinction of species are global challenges that require collective action. Conservationists often work tirelessly to raise awareness about these issues and advocate for international cooperation to address them.

Hoarders, however, may remain focused on their personal possessions to the detriment of broader global concerns. Their worldview can become myopic, and they may not fully grasp the urgency of environmental and social challenges that affect us all. This divergence in perspective underscores the difference in the impact that conservation and hoarding have on the world.

In conclusion, the choices we make regarding the conservation or hoarding of possessions reflect not only our values but also our impact on the world around us. Conservationists serve as guardians of our planet's natural and cultural treasures, working diligently to ensure they endure for generations to come. Theirs is a path of responsibility, stewardship, and interconnectedness.

Hoarders, on the other hand, grapple with a different set of challenges, driven by fear and attachment. While their intentions may be rooted in a desire for security, their actions often lead to isolation, anxiety, and an unhealthy relationship with possessions.

Recognizing the profound difference between conservation and hoarding prompts us to consider our own actions and intentions. It encourages a more thoughtful and sustainable approach to the possessions we hold dear and the impact we have on the world. It is a reminder that the delicate balance between these two perspectives ultimately shapes not only our individual lives but the future of our planet.

CHAPTER TWENTY-SEVEN

Within the Arena: Competition and Ruthlessness Clash

In the grand theater of life, where competition takes center stage, the clash between Competition and Ruthlessness is a perennial narrative, one that resonates with individuals and societies alike. It's a story of conflicting values and divergent strategies, a story that shapes destinies and determines the course of progress.

Competition, as a driving force, embodies the very essence of human ambition. It propels individuals and entities toward greater heights, motivating them to reach for their dreams and aspirations. It is the force behind innovation, the engine of economic growth, and the crucible of evolution itself. In its purest form, competition fosters an environment where hard work, talent, and dedication are rewarded, where meritocracy reigns supreme, and where individuals dare to test the limits of their potential.

On the opposite side of the spectrum stands Ruthlessness, the dark twin of Competition. Ruthlessness takes competition to the extreme, where the pursuit of victory becomes an obsession, and any means are deemed acceptable to achieve the desired ends. Unlike its virtuous counterpart, Ruthlessness recognizes no boundaries, displaying no empathy for collateral damage, be it in the realms of business, sports, or personal relationships. It thrives on manipulation, deceit, and exploitation, leaving behind a wake of discord and chaos.

The paradox here lies in their respective objectives. While Competition seeks progress and growth, Ruthlessness often seeks only self-aggrandizement and dominance. Competition respects rules and fairness, operating within the boundaries of ethical conduct, whereas Ruthlessness sidesteps such principles with impunity. Competition builds bridges, fostering collaboration and innovation, whereas Ruthlessness burns bridges, leaving a trail of broken trust and severed connections in its wake.

In the world of business, Competition serves as a catalyst for companies to continually improve, leading to the creation of better products and services that benefit consumers and society as a whole. It encourages efficiency, customer satisfaction, and the relentless pursuit of excellence. However, when Ruthlessness infiltrates the corporate world, it may resort to unfair trade practices, monopolistic behavior, and unethical tactics that not only stifle competition but also harm the very consumers it purports to serve.

Similarly, in the realm of sports, Competition takes on a sacred aura. It encourages athletes to push their limits, inspiring spectators worldwide with feats of greatness. It exemplifies sportsmanship and camaraderie, uniting people through shared passion and admiration for excellence. But when Ruthlessness infiltrates the arena, it can lead to doping scandals, cheating, and a loss of the game's integrity, disillusioning fans and tarnishing the reputation of the athletes involved.

The crux of this enduring struggle between Competition and Ruthlessness lies in the chosen path. Although both entities share the same arena, it is the approach taken that distinguishes them. Competition champions excellence, fairness, and collaboration, while Ruthlessness thrives on exploitation, deception, and the chaos it sows.

As we navigate the labyrinth of competition in our own lives, it is crucial to recognize this inner battle. It is a choice, a conscious decision we must make, whether to embrace the virtues of Competition or descend into the abyss of Ruthlessness. This choice not only defines our success but also shapes our character and determines the impact we leave on the world.

In this perpetual struggle, let us remember that competition, when harnessed with integrity and purpose, possesses the power to drive progress, inspire innovation, and elevate the human spirit to unprecedented heights. The real competition should not be against others but against our own limitations, motivating us to become the best versions of ourselves while upholding the principles of fairness and compassion.

In the ongoing battle of Competition vs. Ruthlessness, let us aspire to be the champions of a better, more just world—a world where ambition is tempered by empathy, where success is measured not only by what we achieve but by how we achieve it. Let us endeavor to be the authors of a narrative where competition and collaboration coexist harmoniously, where the pursuit of greatness is guided by the moral compass of integrity and the noble aim of advancing the human condition.

In this arena of life, let us collectively architect a brighter future, where Competition, in its purest form, reigns supreme, and Ruthlessness is relegated to the annals of history. Let us recognize that the battle within ourselves is the most significant battle of all, where the choice between these two forces shapes not only our personal destiny but also the trajectory of humanity as a whole.

It is essential to understand that Competition, as an intrinsic part of our existence, extends beyond the individual level. It shapes industries, economies, and even nations. Healthy competition between businesses drives innovation, encourages efficiency, and leads to the development of products and services that benefit society. This form of competition aligns with the principles of fairness and ethics, creating a level playing field where success is determined by merit and customer satisfaction.

However, when Ruthlessness creeps into the corporate world, it can have devastating consequences. Ruthless tactics, such as corporate espionage, price-fixing, or hostile takeovers, can harm not only competitors but also employees, shareholders, and consumers. The pursuit of profit at any cost may lead to unethical decisions that erode trust and tarnish a company's reputation. In the long run, such ruthlessness can destabilize industries and even trigger economic crises.

In the realm of politics and governance, competition between political parties is a fundamental aspect of democratic societies. It allows for the exchange of ideas, promotes accountability, and ensures that leaders are chosen through a fair and transparent process. Healthy political competition can lead to policies that benefit the public, address societal challenges, and protect individual rights.

However, when Ruthlessness infiltrates politics, it can result in divisive tactics, misinformation campaigns, and the erosion of democratic norms. Political leaders who prioritize their personal ambitions over the well-being of their constituents may engage in corrupt practices or undermine the rule of law. Such actions can lead to political polarization, social unrest, and a loss of trust in the democratic system itself.

In our personal lives, the battle between Competition and Ruthlessness is often a reflection of our values and ethics. It influences our relationships, our choices, and our approach to achieving our goals. When we embrace the principles of healthy competition, we strive for excellence while respecting the dignity and rights of others. We seek to collaborate and build bridges, fostering connections that enrich our lives and the lives of those around us.

Conversely, when Ruthlessness takes hold, our pursuit of success can become ruthless and cutthroat. We may prioritize our own interests at the expense of others, resorting to manipulation or deception to achieve our goals. This can lead to strained relationships, a sense of isolation, and a loss of personal integrity.

In the grand tapestry of human history, the struggle between Competition and Ruthlessness has played out in various forms. It has shaped the destinies of empires, influenced the outcomes of wars, and determined the rise and fall of civilizations. Throughout these epochs, societies that have embraced healthy competition, innovation, and collaboration have often thrived and left lasting legacies.

Conversely, societies marked by Ruthlessness, characterized by corruption, exploitation, and the pursuit of power at any cost, have faced internal strife and eventual decline. The lessons of history remind us that the choices we make as individuals and as a collective have profound consequences for the course of our shared human journey.

As we reflect on the enduring battle between Competition and Ruthlessness, let us recognize that it is not a binary choice but a spectrum of possibilities. It is a continuous struggle within ourselves and our societies to strike

a balance between ambition and empathy, between progress and ethical conduct. To navigate this complex landscape, we must cultivate self-awareness, ethical discernment, and a commitment to the common good.

In conclusion, the battle between Competition and Ruthlessness is a timeless narrative that resonates across cultures, industries, and historical epochs. It is a reflection of our human nature, our values, and our aspirations. While competition, when harnessed with integrity and purpose, drives progress, innovation, and human achievement, we must remain vigilant against the allure of Ruthlessness, which can lead to ethical lapses, discord, and the erosion of our shared principles.

As we face this battle within ourselves and within our societies, let us aspire to be champions of a better world—a world where ambition is tempered by empathy, where success is measured not only by what we achieve but by how we achieve it, and where the pursuit of excellence coexists with a commitment to fairness, ethics, and collaboration. In this ongoing struggle, let us strive to be the authors of a narrative that uplifts the human spirit, fosters unity, and paves the way for a brighter and more just future for all.

CHAPTER TWENTY-EIGHT

Crossroads of Giving: Benevolence, Self-Interest, and Charity

In the vast landscape of giving, there exist two distinct and contrasting forces that shape our perceptions and actions: charity, the embodiment of benevolence, and exploitation, the embodiment of opportunism. On the surface, these two forces may seem like polar opposites, their motivations and outcomes starkly divergent. However, beneath the veneer of altruism and self-interest lies a subtle and intricate interplay that challenges our understanding of morality and generosity.

Charity, often seen as a shining beacon of empathy and compassion, is the embodiment of the purest form of giving. It extends its benevolent hand to those in need, representing the noble impulse to alleviate suffering, offering resources, support, and hope to the less fortunate. The intentions behind acts of charity are noble, the motives selfless, and it is this altruistic spirit that makes the world a better place. But even within this virtuous act, there are hidden pitfalls that we must acknowledge.

Exploitation, on the other hand, represents the dark side of human nature—a cunning calculation that capitalizes on vulnerability, seeking personal gain at the expense of others' misfortune. It is the unscrupulous manipulation of the weak for the benefit of the strong. This nefarious aspect of giving tarnishes the very essence of generosity and reflects the shadows that can cast doubt on the purity of human intentions.

Yet, within the intricate dance between charity and exploitation, shades of gray emerge. A charity, for all its good intentions, may inadvertently perpetuate dependency, inadvertently robbing recipients of their self-sufficiency. This paradox raises questions about the long-term impact of charitable acts. Conversely, exploitation, born from self-interest and shadowed motives, may inadvertently trigger societal change, addressing neglected issues in its wake, albeit in a morally questionable manner.

To discern the thin line that separates these dualities requires more than just good intentions; it demands thoughtful actions and a profound understanding of human nature. It calls for an awareness of the potential harm embedded in even the purest of hearts and the potential good hidden in the darkest of motives. This challenge urges us to redefine charity not as a mere handout but as a hand up—an act that empowers those in need to rise from their circumstances and regain their self-sufficiency.

In this exploration, we discover that the true essence of benevolence lies in wisdom—a wisdom that acknowledges the complexity of human nature and the intricacies of human society. It is a wisdom that transforms charity from a superficial gesture into a transformative force for positive change. It is a wisdom that allows us to navigate the thin line between charity and exploitation, ensuring that our actions align with our noblest intentions.

Therefore, as we extend our hands to help others, let us remember that the path to genuine charity is paved with understanding, empathy, and empowerment. It is a path that transcends the dualities of good intentions and hidden agendas, guiding us toward a world where the radiant light of compassion outshines the lingering shadows of exploitation.

In this context, it becomes evident that charity, while driven by the desire to do good, can sometimes inadvertently create a cycle of dependency. When individuals or communities consistently receive aid without opportunities for self-sufficiency or growth, they may become reliant on external support. This unintended consequence raises ethical questions about the long-term impact of charity and whether it truly empowers individuals to improve their lives.

On the other hand, exploitation, with its self-serving motives, can lead to short-term gains for those perpetrating it, but it often comes at the expense of the vulnerable. Exploitation exploits the weaknesses and vulnerabilities of others, perpetuating inequality and suffering. However, in some instances, exploitation may inadvertently shine a light on systemic issues, forcing society to address neglected problems.

To navigate the fine line between charity and exploitation, we must go beyond surface-level intentions. It requires a deep understanding of the complexities of human nature and the societal structures that perpetuate inequality. True charity should not be a mere handout but a means of empowering individuals and communities to break free from cycles of poverty and dependence.

In this exploration, we uncover the importance of wisdom as a guiding force in our charitable endeavors. Wisdom allows us to see beyond the immediate impact of our actions and consider the long-term consequences. It encourages us to seek solutions that address the root causes of suffering and inequality, rather than just addressing the symptoms.

So, as we extend our hands to help others, let us do so with wisdom, empathy, and a commitment to empowerment. Let us remember that the path to genuine charity is not always straightforward and may require us to challenge our own preconceptions and biases. Ultimately, our goal should be to create a world where the radiance of compassion prevails over the shadows of exploitation, where our actions align with our noblest intentions, and where every individual has the opportunity to thrive.

In this ongoing dialogue between charity and exploitation, it is crucial to acknowledge the potential for unintended consequences in our acts of benevolence. When charity is extended without careful consideration, it can inadvertently foster a culture of dependency, where recipients become reliant on external assistance rather than building their own self-sufficiency. This raises important questions about the sustainability and long-term impact of charity.

Exploitation, conversely, often stems from self-interest and the pursuit of personal gain at the expense of others. It can manifest as taking advantage of vulnerable individuals or communities for economic or political reasons. While exploitative actions may yield short-term benefits for the exploiters, they perpetuate inequality and suffering, ultimately eroding the moral fabric of society.

However, there are instances where exploitation inadvertently serves as a catalyst for societal change. It can expose systemic injustices and inequalities, forcing society to confront and address these issues. While the means may be morally questionable, the unintended consequences may lead to positive transformations in the long run.

To navigate the intricate balance between charity and exploitation, we must cultivate a profound wisdom that goes beyond surface-level intentions. Wisdom calls for a deep understanding of human nature, the complexities of social structures, and the multifaceted causes of suffering and inequality. True charity, rooted in wisdom, seeks not only to alleviate immediate needs but also to empower individuals and communities to break free from the cycle of poverty and dependence.

In our pursuit of genuine charity, let us remember that it requires more than good intentions; it demands thoughtful and informed actions. It necessitates empathy, a willingness to challenge our own assumptions, and a commitment to addressing the root causes of suffering. The path to authentic benevolence is one where the light of compassion shines brightly, dispelling the shadows of exploitation, and where our actions align harmoniously with our noblest intentions.

In conclusion, the complex interplay between charity and exploitation challenges our understanding of morality and generosity. While charity represents the noble impulse to alleviate suffering, it can inadvertently perpetuate dependency. Exploitation, on the other hand, capitalizes on vulnerability and self-interest, often leading to short-term gains at the expense of the vulnerable. However, there are instances where exploitation inadvertently exposes societal issues and forces change.

To navigate this delicate balance, wisdom is essential. True charity should empower individuals and communities to rise above their circumstances, addressing the root causes of suffering. As we extend our hands to help others, let us do so with wisdom, empathy, and a commitment to creating a world where the light of compassion outshines the shadows of exploitation.

CHAPTER TWENTY-NINE

Love's Layers: Unmasking the Difference between Love and Infatuation

In matters of the heart, the line between love and infatuation can be deceptively thin. Love, the profound force that binds souls, often stands in stark contrast to its beguiling counterpart, infatuation. On the surface, infatuation wears the guise of passion, yet it conceals a treacherous undertow. Love, with its roots anchored in trust and mutual understanding, takes time to bloom, while infatuation, a swift and fiery spark, blazes brightly but fades fast.

Infatuation wears the cloak of urgency, demanding instant gratification, while love patiently nurtures, allowing bonds to deepen and grow resilient. It thrives on reciprocation, asking little in return, while infatuation can be demanding, seeking constant affirmation. Love listens, hears, and understands; it values individuality and cherishes the essence of a person. Infatuation, however, often reduces its subject to a projection of desires, ignoring complexities for a simplified illusion.

Yet, here lies the paradox: infatuation, while inherently fleeting, can harbor genuine intentions. Beneath its impulsive exterior, it may carry the seeds of true affection, a glimmer of what could blossom into love. Conversely, love, if misunderstood or mismanaged, can turn possessive or stifling, morphing into something that resembles infatuation's darker side.

As we navigate the labyrinth of emotions, it becomes crucial to discern between the allure of infatuation and the steadfast foundation of love. For love, with its patient gaze and unwavering support, is the force that stands the test of time. It endures, weathers storms, and emerges stronger, while infatuation, like a brilliant but fleeting comet, may burn out, leaving only memories of its transient glow.

In this dichotomy, we find the dance of the heart, where both love and infatuation take their turns, teaching us lessons about the depths and shallows of affection. To love is to embrace the imperfections, to understand that passion may ebb and flow, but the core remains steadfast. To be infatuated is to relish the electric spark, knowing it may not last forever but reveling in its intensity nonetheless.

So, let us embark on this exploration, seeking to unravel the enigma of love and infatuation. Let us peel back the layers, acknowledging that within each, there lies a piece of the human experience. For in understanding these intricacies, we come one step closer to comprehending the boundless complexities of the heart.

As the sun sets and rises, so do the tides of our emotions. Love, like a seasoned sailor, navigates these waters with grace and wisdom. It knows that storms will come, but it also knows how to find refuge in the harbor of understanding. Infatuation, on the other hand, is like a tempestuous wave, crashing upon the shore with reckless abandon. It is a force of nature, wild and untamed, but it lacks the depth and nuance that love possesses.

Love is a tapestry woven with threads of trust, respect, and shared dreams. It is a sanctuary where souls find solace in one another. Infatuation, though passionate, often blinds us to the complexities of our partner. It paints a portrait in broad strokes, ignoring the subtle details that make each person a masterpiece in their own right.

In the dance between love and infatuation, we uncover the symphony of human connection. Love is the steady bassline, grounding us in a rhythm of mutual respect and admiration. Infatuation is the crescendo, a burst of energy that electrifies our senses. Together, they compose a melody that tells the story of our hearts.

Love gazes into the future with hopeful eyes, envisioning a life intertwined with another. It is a partnership forged in the fires of adversity and tempered by shared triumphs. Infatuation, though exhilarating, often lives in the present moment, intoxicated by the immediate thrill. It may struggle to envision a future beyond the intoxicating rush it provides.

In the realms of love and infatuation, vulnerability takes center stage. Love encourages us to bare our souls, to reveal our true selves without fear of judgment. Infatuation, while passionate, can sometimes shy away from the depths of true intimacy, content with the surface-level connection it provides.

Love is a garden, carefully tended and nurtured, where the blossoms of affection bloom in their own time. Infatuation is a wildfire, consuming everything in its path with a fierce and indiscriminate heat. Both have their place in the landscape of human connection, but recognizing their distinct nature allows us to navigate these territories with wisdom and grace.

To love is to embark on a journey, knowing that the path may be winding and at times challenging, but finding solace in the companionship of another soul. To be infatuated is to revel in the whirlwind, to let oneself be carried away by the intoxicating rush of emotions. Each holds its own allure, but it is in understanding their unique qualities that we can truly appreciate the spectrum of human experience.

Love, with its roots sunk deep into the soil of trust, withstands the test of time and weathers even the harshest of storms. It is a sanctuary, a safe haven where hearts find refuge. Infatuation, while passionate and exhilarating, can be a fleeting flame, burning brightly but quickly fading into the night.

In the dance of love and infatuation, we come to realize that both have their place in the grand tapestry of our lives. They are the contrasting strokes of color that give depth and dimension to our emotional landscape. To love deeply is to know oneself and to be known in return. To be infatuated is to lose oneself momentarily in the intoxicating rush of desire.

Ultimately, it is through experiencing both love and infatuation that we come to understand the full spectrum of our hearts. Each teaches us invaluable lessons about connection, desire, and the complexities of human emotions. As we navigate these territories, let us do so with open hearts and discerning minds, embracing the beauty and depth that both love and infatuation offer. For in this exploration, we uncover the true essence of what it means to be human.

The heart, that enigmatic organ that guides our emotions, is a realm of paradoxes and mysteries. It beats with both the steady rhythm of love's devotion and the erratic tempo of infatuation's intoxication. At times, we may find ourselves standing at the crossroads, torn between the enduring embrace of love and the fleeting allure of infatuation.

Love, like a finely aged wine, matures with time. It deepens, becoming a well of strength and stability upon which we can rely. Love is the whisper of reassurance in the darkest of nights, the unwavering hand that reaches out to catch us when we stumble. It is the force that binds generations, creating a tapestry of interconnected lives.

Infatuation, on the other hand, is the shooting star in the night sky, a brilliant burst of passion that momentarily lights up our world. It is the rush of adrenaline, the racing heart, the butterflies in our stomachs. Infatuation can sweep us off our feet, leaving us breathless and exhilarated, but it is often as transient as the fleeting comet's tail.

Love is the anchor that keeps us grounded, allowing us to weather life's tempests together. It is a dance of two souls, moving in harmony, supporting each other's steps. Love requires patience, understanding, and compromise. It thrives on the beauty of imperfection, finding strength in vulnerability.

Infatuation, on the other hand, can be intoxicating precisely because it is uncomplicated. It is the spark that ignites with a glance, the passion that burns brightly in the early stages of a relationship. Infatuation is the embodiment of desire, the rush of attraction that leaves us longing for more.

Yet, it is essential to recognize that infatuation, while thrilling, can also be deceiving. It can blind us to red flags and flaws in our partner, leading us to idealize them. Love, on the other hand, sees the flaws and imperfections and loves despite them. It is the choice to stand by someone's side, even when the initial fervor has waned.

In the spectrum of emotions, love and infatuation are two sides of the same coin, both offering unique experiences and insights into the human heart. Love is the patient gardener, nurturing the seeds of affection and watching them bloom over time. Infatuation is the spontaneous fireworks display, a dazzling spectacle that leaves us awestruck.

As we navigate the complexities of love and infatuation, it is essential to recognize the difference between the two. Love is built on a foundation of trust, respect, and deep connection. It is a partnership that endures and evolves with time. Infatuation, while passionate, can be shallow and fleeting, often driven by external appearances and superficial attractions.

The journey of love is a marathon, not a sprint. It is a commitment to standing by someone's side through life's ups and downs. It is the willingness to grow and evolve together, to weather the storms, and to celebrate the victories. Infatuation, in contrast, is the sprinter's burst of energy, intense but short-lived.

In the grand tapestry of our lives, both love and infatuation play crucial roles. Love is the anchor that keeps us grounded, while infatuation is the gust of wind that can lift us to dizzying heights. Each offers its own unique beauty, but it is in the understanding of their differences that we find wisdom.

So, let us continue our exploration of the heart's intricacies, embracing the richness and depth of both love and infatuation. In doing so, we come one step closer to unraveling the enigma of human emotion and connection, finding meaning in the delicate balance between the enduring and the ephemeral.

CHAPTER THIRTY

Time's Tide: Navigating Tradition and Stagnation

In the grand tapestry of human history, the juxtaposition of Tradition and Stagnation emerges as an intricate and ever-evolving theme. These two tributaries of the river of time possess their own unique characters, shaping the destinies of civilizations and the course of humanity's journey. Tradition, much like the unwavering current of the river, flows with a sense of continuity, forging connections to our ancestral roots. It carries with it the collective wisdom of countless generations, the harmonious melodies of cultural legacies, and the comforting embrace of age-old customs. Tradition is the embodiment of rituals that weave the tapestry of our shared identity, reminding us of our origins and the path we've trodden.

Amidst this steady current, however, the murky waters of Stagnation loom ominously. These stagnant backwaters are characterized by an immobilizing resistance to change, their depths choked with the debris of outdated beliefs, unyielding dogmas, and an apprehension of the unfamiliar. Stagnation embodies a sense of complacency that clings stubbornly to the familiar, even when its relevance to our evolving needs has waned. It represents a reluctance to relinquish the grip of the past, imprisoning us in antiquated paradigms.

Tradition, at its core, seeks to provide a profound sense of belonging and identity. It offers a cultural anchor, a tapestry intricately woven with the threads of history and shared experiences. It is the source of cultural pride, fostering unity and kinship among communities worldwide. Yet, Tradition is not without its flaws. Sometimes, in its unyielding commitment to preserving customs, it can inadvertently veer into oppressive or discriminatory territory. The genuine warmth of cultural celebration can metamorphose into a cold, unyielding conformity that stifles progress and restricts individual liberties.

Conversely, Stagnation, though often criticized for its obstinacy, may harbor noble intentions. It resists change not out of malevolence but due to a genuine concern for stability and the preservation of a community's core values. It sees itself as a guardian of cultural heritage, endeavoring to protect what it deems indispensable. However, this noble aspiration can lead to stagnation's quagmire, where progress languishes and innovation remains suppressed.

The question that looms before us is how to navigate this confluence of Tradition and Stagnation in the river of time. How can we ensure that Tradition retains its heartwarming qualities while steering clear of Stagnation's icy grip? The answer lies in our role as discerning stewards of our cultural heritage. We must cherish the aspects of Tradition that foster unity and identity, infusing them with the vitality of adaptation and inclusivity. We must be vigilant, recognizing when Tradition inadvertently leads us into Stagnation's treacherous waters, and summon the courage to chart a new course when necessary.

In the end, Tradition and Stagnation are not starkly opposing forces but rather intertwined currents, inviting us to find a delicate equilibrium. It is a dance along the riverbanks of time, where we honor our past while eagerly embracing the future. It is a journey in which we celebrate our roots while extending our reach toward new horizons. This journey calls for wisdom, empathy, and an unwavering commitment to progress without forsaking our cherished identity.

As the river of time flows ceaselessly, it is incumbent upon us to ensure that Tradition remains a source of strength and unity. We must guide it, like a skilled captain, toward a brighter future, free from the stagnation born of fear and complacency. In this endeavor, we discover the true artistry of navigating the river of time, striking a harmonious chord between our past and our future, ensuring that the currents of Tradition and Stagnation propel us toward a destiny that is rich in both heritage and progress.

In our journey to navigate these intricate waters, it is essential to recognize that Tradition is not a static entity but a living, breathing force. It evolves with the times, absorbing new influences while retaining its core essence. Like a river that reshapes its course over centuries, Tradition can adapt and remain relevant without losing its authenticity. It is in this adaptability that Tradition finds its true strength, bridging the gap between generations and allowing cultures to thrive in a dynamic world.

Moreover, Tradition should be a wellspring of inspiration rather than a source of rigidity. It can serve as a platform for innovation, offering a stable foundation from which creative ideas can flourish. When Tradition and innovation dance together, they create a vibrant synergy that propels societies forward while honoring their heritage.

Conversely, Stagnation, when unchecked, can lead to the erosion of the very values it seeks to protect. It can become a barrier to progress, stifling the growth of ideas and the exploration of new frontiers. In this sense, Stagnation can be seen as a treacherous undertow, pulling societies into a quagmire of mediocrity and inertia.

To navigate these complex waters successfully, we must foster open dialogues that bridge the gap between Tradition and the imperative for change. We must encourage respectful discourse that allows us to reevaluate customs that no longer serve us while preserving those that anchor us to our cultural heritage. It is through these dialogues that we can find common ground, fostering a sense of shared purpose in the face of evolving challenges.

In our quest to strike a balance between Tradition and Stagnation, it is crucial to recognize that no culture exists in isolation. In our interconnected world, cultures constantly influence and shape one another. This interplay of ideas, customs, and traditions is a testament to the dynamic nature of human society. It reminds us that we are all co-travelers on this ever-flowing river of time, learning from one another's experiences and enriching our own heritage in the process.

Ultimately, Tradition and Stagnation are not two opposing forces but rather a spectrum along which cultures navigate. This spectrum allows societies to find their unique equilibrium, adapting to the challenges of the present while preserving the wisdom of the past. It is a delicate dance, a continuous dialogue between the old and the new, the familiar and the unknown.

In conclusion, as we journey along the river of time, we must recognize that Tradition and Stagnation are not fixed points but rather dynamic currents that ebb and flow. Our role as stewards of this river is to ensure that Tradition remains a source of strength and unity, steering clear of Stagnation's icy grip. It is a journey that demands our unwavering commitment to progress while honoring our cherished identity. In this delicate balancing act, we find the true artistry of navigating the river of time, forging a path toward a future that is both rooted in heritage and enriched by innovation.

CHAPTER THIRTY-ONE

Moral Maze: Navigating Mentorship and Manipulation

In the realm of guidance and influence, there exists a fine line—one that often blurs the boundary between noble intentions and questionable means. This is the line between mentorship and manipulation.

Mentorship is the embodiment of wisdom, born from a sincere desire to nurture the growth and development of others. It's the guiding light that helps individuals find their own path, offering insights, sharing experiences, and bestowing the invaluable gift of knowledge. A mentor empowers, uplifts, and imparts the tools for independent thinking and decision-making. In its purest form, mentorship is the beacon of genuine support.

On the opposite end of this spectrum is manipulation, the dark art of influencing others to serve one's own agenda, often at their expense. It's the subtle coercion that preys on vulnerabilities, the deceptive charm that disguises ulterior motives. Manipulation exploits trust and goodwill for personal gain, sowing confusion, self-doubt, and dependency. It's a betrayal of the very essence of mentorship—guidance stripped of authenticity.

But here's where the paradox unfolds. Sometimes, even within the realm of manipulation, there exists an agenda that, in isolation, may seem noble. The manipulator might genuinely believe that their actions, while deceitful, serve a greater good. They convince themselves that the ends justify the means, a dangerous justification that echoes through history's darker chapters.

Conversely, in mentorship, the best of intentions can occasionally pave the road to unintended consequences. A mentor's unwavering belief in their own perspective can inadvertently stifle independent thought in their mentee, creating a reliance that hinders growth rather than nurturing it.

So, how do we navigate this moral maze? The key lies in awareness and discernment. To recognize the stark difference between genuine mentorship and manipulation, one must cultivate a critical eye and an open mind.

Ask questions. Examine the motivations behind guidance. Evaluate whether the path illuminated by another empowers you or subtly chains you. Consider the long-term effects of the relationship. Is it fostering independence and growth, or is it fostering dependency and manipulation?

In the intricate dance between mentorship and manipulation, our moral compasses guide us. They remind us that even the noblest of agendas can be tainted by unethical means, and that the true essence of mentorship is not just in the destination but in the journey, one that should empower, not manipulate, the seeker of wisdom.

In this dance of guidance, it's imperative to acknowledge the vulnerability inherent in the search for wisdom. Both the mentor and the manipulated must recognize that trust is the cornerstone of this relationship. Trust is the fragile thread that, once broken, may never fully mend. It is the mentor's solemn duty to honor this trust with integrity, refraining from veering into the treacherous terrain of manipulation.

Furthermore, true mentorship recognizes the individuality of each seeker. It is a tailored approach, acknowledging that one size does not fit all. A mentor understands that their role is not to mold a mentee into a mirror image, but to help them unearth their unique potential and strengths.

In contrast, manipulation often operates from a place of ego, where the manipulator seeks to shape others in their own likeness, disregarding the mentee's distinct journey. This self-serving agenda erodes the very foundation of genuine mentorship, replacing it with a hollow facade.

Moreover, transparency is the bedrock of mentorship. A mentor willingly shares their own experiences, including their missteps and failures. This vulnerability serves to humanize the mentor, demonstrating that wisdom is a product of a journey, not an innate trait. It encourages the mentee to embrace their own imperfections, fostering an environment of growth.

In manipulation, transparency is conspicuously absent. The manipulator shrouds their true intentions, weaving a web of half-truths and carefully crafted narratives. This deceit erodes the trust that should be the cornerstone of any meaningful mentor-mentee relationship.

As we traverse the terrain of mentorship and manipulation, it's crucial to recognize that the journey is not always linear. There may be moments of doubt and ambiguity, where the distinction between the two becomes blurred. It is in these moments that introspection and reflection become invaluable tools.

Ultimately, the measure of a mentor's legacy lies not in the number of followers they amass, but in the depth of impact they leave behind. It is in the mentees who, having been guided with integrity, go on to illuminate their own paths and uplift others in turn.

In contrast, the legacy of manipulation is one of broken trust, of hollow victories built on the backs of deceived souls. It leaves a trail of shattered potential and stifled growth in its wake.

In this intricate tapestry of guidance, let us remember that true mentorship is a sacred trust—a torch passed from one seeker of wisdom to another. It is a legacy of empowerment, of nurturing the flames of potential until they burn brightly on their own.

And in the face of manipulation, let us stand resolute, armed with the awareness to discern the shadows that seek to dim our light. Let us remember that our journey towards wisdom should never come at the cost of our autonomy and authenticity.

To further understand the delicate balance between mentorship and manipulation, it is essential to delve into the psychology behind these actions. Mentorship, at its core, is rooted in empathy and a genuine desire to uplift others. It is about recognizing the potential in someone and offering guidance to help them reach their full capabilities. This requires a deep understanding of the mentee's needs, aspirations, and struggles.

Manipulation, on the other hand, often springs from a more self-centered place. It may begin with a desire for power, control, or personal gain. Manipulators are skilled at reading people, but their insights are used not to empower but to exploit. They prey on vulnerabilities, capitalizing on weaknesses to further their own agendas.

In mentorship, the relationship is built on trust and respect. A mentor creates a safe space for the mentee to express their thoughts and feelings, free from judgment. This fosters open communication and the free exchange of ideas. The mentor's goal is to nurture the mentee's self-esteem and self-efficacy, helping them develop the confidence to make their own decisions.

In contrast, manipulation thrives in an environment of secrecy and deception. Manipulators often employ tactics designed to keep their targets off balance. They may use gaslighting techniques to make the victim doubt their own perceptions or employ guilt trips and emotional manipulation to gain compliance. The result is a toxic dynamic built on fear and control.

Understanding the underlying motivations behind mentorship and manipulation is essential for both mentors and mentees. It allows mentors to stay true to their noble intentions and avoid slipping into manipulative behavior, even unintentionally. It also equips mentees with the knowledge to recognize when they are being manipulated and to seek healthier, more empowering relationships.

It is worth noting that the line between mentorship and manipulation is not always clear-cut. There may be instances where a mentor genuinely believes they are acting in the best interest of the mentee but inadvertently employs manipulative tactics. Similarly, a manipulator may mask their intentions under the guise of mentorship. This complexity underscores the importance of constant self-reflection and ethical evaluation in these relationships.

In the digital age, where information flows freely and influence can be wielded from behind a screen, the dynamics of mentorship and manipulation have taken on new dimensions. Social media platforms, for example, have become fertile grounds for both genuine mentors and manipulative influencers.

True mentors on social media share their knowledge openly, engage with their followers respectfully, and encourage critical thinking. They understand that their influence carries a responsibility to promote ethical behavior and positive values.

Manipulators on social media, however, often prioritize personal gain, whether in the form of followers, likes, or financial benefits. They may use clickbait tactics, sensationalism, and emotional appeals to capture attention and draw people into their web of influence. These manipulative practices erode the authenticity and trust that should underpin online mentorship.

As we navigate the intricate web of mentorship and manipulation in the digital age, it becomes crucial to exercise digital literacy and critical thinking skills. We must be discerning consumers of information and influence, carefully evaluating the motives and credibility of those we choose to follow and emulate.

In conclusion, the fine line between mentorship and manipulation underscores the complexity of human relationships and the ethical considerations that accompany them. Mentorship, when grounded in empathy and authenticity, can be a powerful force for personal and societal growth. In contrast, manipulation, driven by self-interest and deceit, erodes trust and stifles individual potential.

To walk this fine line with integrity, we must cultivate self-awareness, empathy, and critical thinking. We must recognize that the true essence of mentorship lies not in control but in empowerment, and that manipulation, no matter how well-intentioned it may seem, is a betrayal of trust and authenticity. In embracing the principles of genuine mentorship, we can guide others toward their fullest potential while upholding the values of ethics and empathy that define the noble path.

CHAPTER THIRTY-TWO

Conflict's Crossroads: Finding the Balance between Passivity and Aversion

In the realm of interpersonal dynamics, we often grapple with the age-old question of when to hold our peace and when to stand up for our principles. It's a delicate tightrope walk between two seemingly contrasting aspects: passivity and aversion to conflict. On one side, we have the passive individual, someone who avoids confrontation at any cost, seeking harmony but sometimes neglecting their own needs. On the other, we find the person with an aversion to conflict, someone who readily engages in disputes, believing that it's the path to justice, yet potentially fueling unnecessary tension.

The passive individual might be seen as the epitome of tranquility, a soothing presence in a world often marred by strife. They strive for peace, are empathetic listeners, and avoid rocking the boat. However, their passivity can often morph into a cloak of invisibility, where their voice goes unheard, their needs unmet, and their values sacrificed for the sake of harmony.

On the flip side, the conflict-averse person champions their cause with vigor, refusing to let injustices slide and fighting for what they believe in. Admirably, they are unafraid to address issues head-on, but this approach can sometimes lead to collateral damage—strained relationships, burned bridges, and emotional exhaustion.

The essence of finding a balance between these dualities lies in recognizing that both aspects have merits and pitfalls. The passive individual can benefit from assertiveness training, learning to express their needs and beliefs without fear of discord. Meanwhile, the conflict-averse can adopt a more diplomatic approach, seeking compromise and collaboration as alternatives to outright confrontation.

It is in this nuanced dance between passivity and aversion to conflict that we find the sweet spot—a place where one can prioritize peace and justice simultaneously. The path to effective communication and harmony often involves acknowledging when to be passive and when to confront, recognizing that conflict isn't inherently negative, but rather a means to mutual understanding and growth. So, let us embrace the wisdom of balance, where one can be strong in their convictions yet flexible in their approach, and where harmony is not the absence of conflict but the art of resolving it constructively.

Within this dynamic interplay of passivity and aversion to conflict, we encounter the profound interconnection of these two aspects of human nature. Passivity, in its purest form, often emanates from a genuine desire to maintain harmony and promote a peaceful coexistence. Those who embody this trait are often excellent listeners, empathetic souls who strive to create an atmosphere of serenity around them. However, this noble pursuit of peace can sometimes lead them down a path of self-neglect, where their own desires and principles take a backseat to the collective comfort.

On the opposing end of this spectrum lies the individual with an aversion to conflict, a warrior for justice who refuses to let transgressions go unaddressed. This person's unwavering commitment to addressing issues head-on is undeniably admirable, as they believe that confrontation is a direct route to rectifying wrongs. Yet, this zealous pursuit of justice can inadvertently sow discord and estrangement in relationships, creating emotional minefields that needlessly drain their energy.

Finding the equilibrium necessitates self-awareness and discernment. It involves recognizing the situations where passivity can be a source of strength, allowing for patience and understanding to prevail. Simultaneously, it calls for the wisdom to discern when conflicts need to be confronted, as they often serve as catalysts for growth and transformation.

At the heart of this delicate balance is the belief that harmony can coexist with conflict, and in fact, the two can complement each other. Constructive conflict, when approached with empathy and a shared goal of resolution, can lead to deeper understanding and stronger connections. It is not about avoiding conflict at all costs or seeking it out needlessly, but rather about navigating it skillfully when it arises.

Embracing this wisdom allows individuals to cultivate the art of resilience, where they stand unwavering in their principles yet remain open to dialogue and compromise. It is a testament to the human capacity to evolve and adapt, finding strength in vulnerability and unity in diversity. In this delicate balance, we discover not only the path to harmonious relationships but also the key to personal growth and fulfillment.

Passivity and aversion to conflict are not static traits; they exist on a fluid continuum that can be navigated with intention and self-awareness. The passive individual can learn to assert themselves when necessary, ensuring that their voice is heard and their values upheld without compromising their pursuit of peace. Likewise, the conflict-averse individual can refine their approach, recognizing that diplomacy and collaboration can be powerful tools in achieving justice and resolution.

In the tapestry of human interaction, the threads of passivity and aversion to conflict are woven together, creating a rich and intricate pattern of relationships. Each thread contributes its unique texture and color, and it is in the skillful blending of these elements that we find the beauty of balance.

Ultimately, the quest for balance between passivity and aversion to conflict is a journey of self-discovery and growth. It requires a deep understanding of one's own values, needs, and boundaries, as well as a willingness to engage with others in a spirit of empathy and cooperation. It is a journey that leads to not only healthier relationships but also a greater sense of inner peace and fulfillment.

In conclusion, the delicate dance between passivity and aversion to conflict is an art that requires finesse and wisdom. It is a journey of self-discovery and growth, where individuals learn to assert themselves when necessary and embrace diplomacy and collaboration as tools for resolution. In this balance, we find the harmony between peace and justice, and the path to both personal and interpersonal fulfillment.

Finding the middle ground between passivity and aversion to conflict also involves understanding that these tendencies can be situational. There are times when passivity serves as the wisest course of action, allowing for the de-escalation of tense situations and the preservation of relationships. On the other hand, there are moments when confronting issues head-on is necessary to ensure that justice prevails and boundaries are respected.

Moreover, it's crucial to acknowledge that these traits can coexist within the same individual, manifesting differently depending on the context. A person may be passive in their personal life but assertive in their professional endeavors, demonstrating the adaptability and complexity of human behavior.

To strike this delicate balance, individuals can benefit from cultivating emotional intelligence and effective communication skills. Emotional intelligence helps in recognizing and managing one's own emotions as well as understanding the emotions of others, which is essential for navigating conflicts with empathy and sensitivity.

Effective communication, on the other hand, is the bridge that connects passivity and conflict aversion. It involves the art of expressing one's thoughts, needs, and concerns in a clear and respectful manner, while also actively listening to others. By honing these skills, individuals can navigate the fine line between passivity and conflict aversion, ensuring that they stand up for their values and needs while also promoting understanding and harmony in their relationships.

In the grand tapestry of human interaction, finding the balance between passivity and aversion to conflict is akin to creating a masterpiece. It requires patience, practice, and a deep understanding of oneself and others. It's a journey of personal growth and self-discovery, where individuals learn to harness the strengths of both passivity and conflict aversion while mitigating their respective weaknesses.

Ultimately, the pursuit of this balance is not a destination but an ongoing process. It's a continuous effort to refine one's approach to interpersonal dynamics, to recognize when to yield and when to stand firm, and to navigate the ever-shifting currents of human relationships with grace and wisdom.

In the end, the true artistry lies in being able to adapt and respond to each unique situation, to recognize that the interplay between passivity and aversion to conflict is as varied and complex as the colors on an artist's palette. It's a reminder that human relationships are a living canvas, ever-evolving and infinitely rich, and that the pursuit of balance within them is a journey well worth undertaking.

CHAPTER THIRTY-THREE

Change's Chorus: Balancing Adaptability and Fickleness

In the grand theater of life, we often find ourselves spectators and actors in the eternal drama of adaptability and fickleness. These two facets of human nature are like twin siblings, seemingly born of the same parents—change and uncertainty—yet separated by a thin line that often blurs before our eyes.

Consider adaptability, the virtuous twin. It is the ability to pivot gracefully in the face of change, to dance with the shifting winds of circumstance. Adaptability whispers tales of survival and evolution, where those who embrace it thrive in a world that is ever-shifting. It is the trait of the agile entrepreneur who turns adversity into opportunity, the resilient soul who weathers life's storms with grace.

Yet, lurking in the shadows is fickleness, the mischievous twin. It masquerades as adaptability but wears a different mask. Fickleness is the art of change without purpose, a chameleon without a cause. It dances from one passion to the next, one commitment to another, leaving a trail of unfinished projects and broken promises. Fickleness pretends to be adaptable, but it is the unreliable friend who constantly shifts allegiances without rhyme or reason.

The line that divides these twins can be elusive. At what point does adaptability turn into fickleness, and vice versa? Is it when change becomes a habit rather than a necessity? Or when commitment wanes as quickly as it blooms?

Perhaps the answer lies in the intention behind the change. Adaptability, at its core, serves a purpose—a better life, a more profound understanding, a higher goal. It is the student who switches majors to pursue their true passion, the couple who adapt to the complexities of a long-term relationship, and the society that evolves to embrace diversity and progress.

On the other hand, fickleness lacks a higher purpose. It changes for the sake of change, driven by novelty rather than necessity. It is the consumer who discards last year's gadget for the latest model, the employee who hops from job to job seeking an elusive "perfect fit," and the friend who drifts away when the going gets tough.

As we navigate the delicate balance between these twins, let us remember the importance of intention and purpose. Change is not inherently good or bad; it is a force of nature. What matters is how we harness it. Adaptability is the key to progress, a bridge to new horizons. Fickleness, when left unchecked, becomes a never-ending loop of dissatisfaction.

In this eternal tug of war between adaptability and fickleness, let us strive for change with purpose, for adaptation with a clear vision. Let us be the architects of our destinies, navigating the seas of change with a steady hand on the tiller, charting a course towards a brighter tomorrow. In doing so, we harness the virtuous twin and silence the mischievous one, finding the balance that defines the art of change in the human experience.

Adaptability, in its truest form, is the embodiment of growth and resilience. It's the quality that enables individuals and societies to respond to challenges, learn from experiences, and emerge stronger. Think of a tree that bends with the wind rather than resisting it. Such adaptability allows it to survive the harshest storms.

Conversely, fickleness is a fleeting muse that leads us astray. It tempts us with the allure of constant novelty, urging us to abandon the path we've chosen for the allure of the unknown. However, it rarely offers lasting fulfillment, leaving us perpetually unsatisfied and disconnected from our deeper aspirations.

To truly understand the dichotomy between these twins, we must recognize that adaptability requires a foundation of stability. It's the ability to pivot while still holding onto core values and goals. It's the capacity to embrace change without losing sight of the purpose that drives us. In contrast, fickleness lacks this stability, often leading to a sense of aimlessness and dissatisfaction.

The challenge lies in striking a balance between these two twins. We must cultivate adaptability as a cornerstone of personal growth and progress, using it to navigate the unpredictable waters of life. Yet, we must also be wary of succumbing to fickleness, which can lead to a scattered existence devoid of depth and meaning.

One way to achieve this balance is through mindfulness. By regularly evaluating our motives for change and the impact of our decisions, we can discern whether we are acting out of adaptability or succumbing to fickleness. This self-awareness enables us to make choices that align with our long-term goals and values.

Moreover, adaptability is a skill that can be honed over time. It involves developing resilience, emotional intelligence, and the ability to learn from setbacks. It requires the courage to embrace change while remaining steadfast in our commitment to personal growth and the betterment of society.

In essence, adaptability and fickleness represent two sides of the same coin. They remind us that change is inevitable and that our response to it defines our journey. While adaptability enriches our lives with wisdom and growth, fickleness serves as a cautionary tale, warning us against the allure of fleeting whims.

In conclusion, the interplay between adaptability and fickleness is a timeless theme in the human experience. It challenges us to cultivate the former while resisting the temptations of the latter. By embracing change with intention and purpose, we can harness the virtuous twin and navigate the intricate dance of life with grace and fulfillment, finding our way to a brighter and more meaningful future.

CHAPTER THIRTY-FOUR

Selfless Scales: Balancing Sacrifice and Martyrdom

In the realm of selflessness and devotion, two contrasting forces often emerge: sacrifice and martyrdom. At first glance, they may seem like two sides of the same noble coin, both driven by a profound commitment to a cause or an ideal. However, a deeper examination reveals the subtle yet critical distinctions that set them apart.

Sacrifice, the act of willingly giving up something of value for a greater good, is a hallmark of empathy and compassion. It represents the essence of altruism, where individuals prioritize the welfare of others over their own desires or comforts. Sacrifice is the hand that reaches out to lift others up, the silent heroism that goes unnoticed by many but enriches the lives of those it touches. It is an embodiment of love, kindness, and selflessness.

On the other hand, martyrdom carries a different, more complex connotation. While it too involves self-sacrifice, martyrdom often implies a willingness to endure suffering, even to the point of death, for a higher purpose or belief. It is the act of making a profound statement, often a defiant one, in the face of oppression, injustice, or persecution. Martyrs become symbols of resistance and unwavering commitment, inspiring others to carry the torch of their cause.

However, the distinction between these two concepts lies in the approach and the consequences. Sacrifice, while selfless, generally aims to create positive change or alleviate suffering without the expectation of personal gain or recognition. It operates from a place of empathy and love, seeking to build bridges and mend wounds.

Martyrdom, on the other hand, can be seen as an extreme manifestation of selflessness, but it often carries a weighty cost. It may lead to violence, division, and further suffering, as it is frequently an act of defiance against an oppressive force. The good agenda that underlies martyrdom may become clouded by the collateral damage it incurs.

So, the question arises: Can we maintain the noble intent of sacrifice while avoiding the pitfalls of martyrdom? Can we make our selfless acts resonate with positive change and harmony rather than conflict and suffering?

Perhaps the answer lies in recognizing that selflessness need not be a path of suffering or defiance. It can be a beacon of hope and transformation, a force that unites rather than divides. By channeling our selflessness into acts of love, compassion, and understanding, we can create a world where sacrifice is not a painful struggle but a joyful contribution to the greater good.

It is essential to remember that sacrifice, when carried out with genuine empathy, can be a powerful force for good. The selflessness embedded in acts of sacrifice can uplift communities, heal wounds, and bring about positive change. It's the parent who sacrifices personal ambitions to provide a better life for their children, the healthcare worker who tirelessly cares for patients, or the volunteer who dedicates time to a charitable cause. These acts of sacrifice embody the best of humanity, demonstrating that we can put the needs of others before our own without fanfare or martyrdom.

Martyrdom, on the other hand, often emerges in situations of extreme injustice or oppression. Those who choose this path are willing to endure suffering and even sacrifice their lives to shed light on profound systemic problems. Their actions serve as a rallying cry for change and a testament to the indomitable spirit of human resolve. Think of figures like Mahatma Gandhi, Martin Luther King Jr., and countless others who took a stand against oppression, knowing the personal risks involved.

However, it's crucial to recognize that martyrdom is not without its complexities and potential pitfalls. The sacrifices made in the name of martyrdom can sometimes be viewed as provocative or divisive, leading to unintended consequences. In some cases, martyrdom can even be co-opted by those who seek to perpetuate violence or extremism. Therefore, the decision to tread the path of martyrdom requires careful consideration of the broader context and the potential ramifications.

In our quest for selflessness, we must strike a balance between sacrifice and martyrdom. While sacrifice embodies the everyday acts of kindness and compassion that make our communities stronger, martyrdom calls us to confront systemic injustices and oppressive forces. The key lies in understanding when each approach is most appropriate and effective.

Moreover, as individuals and societies, we should continually strive to create environments where sacrifice is valued and martyrdom becomes less necessary. By addressing social injustices, fostering empathy, and working collectively to build a fairer and more compassionate world, we can reduce the need for extreme acts of selflessness.

In conclusion, the realms of sacrifice and martyrdom represent two facets of our capacity for selflessness and devotion. Sacrifice, when driven by empathy and kindness, can bring about positive change and uplift those in need. Martyrdom, while a powerful symbol of resistance, must be approached with caution, recognizing its potential complexities and consequences. To navigate this complex landscape, we must find a balance that honors both the everyday heroes of sacrifice and the trailblazers of martyrdom, all in the pursuit of a more compassionate and harmonious world.

The essence of sacrifice is deeply rooted in human history and culture. Across generations and societies, we find stories of individuals who willingly gave up their own comfort, safety, or possessions to help others. From the heroic tales of firefighters rushing into burning buildings to save lives to the selfless act of a stranger paying for someone's groceries in a time of need, sacrifice is a universal language of compassion.

In literature and mythology, characters who embody sacrifice often serve as inspirational figures. Consider the story of Frodo Baggins in J.R.R. Tolkien's "The Lord of the Rings." He embarks on a perilous journey to destroy the One Ring, fully aware of the personal sacrifices he must make to save Middle-earth from darkness. Frodo's courage and willingness to endure suffering for the greater good resonate deeply with readers, reminding us of the power of selflessness.

Martyrdom, too, has left an indelible mark on human history. Figures like Joan of Arc, who faced persecution and death for her beliefs, or Socrates, who chose to drink hemlock rather than compromise his principles, are remembered as martyrs who stood firm in their convictions. Their sacrifices have shaped the course of history and inspired countless others to uphold their values even in the face of adversity.

However, it is essential to tread carefully when considering the path of martyrdom. While the courage and commitment of martyrs are undeniable, the consequences of their actions can be unpredictable. The sacrifices made may not always lead to the intended change or result in the betterment of society. The line between martyrdom and extremism can be thin, and the risk of unintentional harm looms large.

To strike a balance between sacrifice and martyrdom, we must recognize that selflessness does not require us to court suffering or defy authority at all costs. Instead, it calls for empathy, compassion, and a thoughtful approach to helping others. Acts of sacrifice can range from small daily kindnesses to significant life choices that prioritize the well-being of others.

Furthermore, in our pursuit of a more compassionate world, it is essential to engage in constructive dialogue and peaceful advocacy to address injustices and systemic problems. While martyrdom has its place in history, it should not be the default response to oppression or injustice. Instead, we can draw inspiration from martyrs' unwavering commitment to their beliefs while seeking peaceful avenues for change that minimize harm and division.

In conclusion, the concepts of sacrifice and martyrdom reflect the profound depths of human selflessness and devotion. Sacrifice,

rooted in empathy and kindness, has the power to uplift individuals and communities. Martyrdom, while historically significant, must be approached with caution, considering the broader consequences of such acts. By finding a balance between these two forces and fostering a culture of compassion, we can collectively work towards a more harmonious world where selflessness shines as a beacon of hope and transformation without the need for extreme sacrifices.

CHAPTER THIRTY-FIVE

Tightrope of Identity: Navigating Community and Conformity

In the delicate balance between community and conformity, we encounter the very essence of our collective existence—a profound and timeless theme that has echoed through human history. This intricate interplay of forces forms the backdrop of our social landscapes, shaping our identities, relationships, and the course of our shared journey through life.

Community, a beacon of warmth and belonging, beckons us with its embrace. It is the tapestry of shared values and aspirations that binds us together, creating a sanctuary where like-minded souls find solace and connection. Within the loving confines of community, we discover the profound significance of kinship, the strength of unity, and the magic of finding our place in a larger whole. It provides a source of identity, a wellspring of support, and a repository of shared experiences that enrich our lives.

However, even within this nurturing embrace, there exists the potential for a double-edged sword. The bonds that unite us can become constricting, and the sanctuary may transform into a stifling enclosure. The very values that form the foundation of our community may, on occasion, become a source of exclusion and division. The challenge arises when our sense of belonging metamorphoses into blind conformity, when our community demands homogeneity at the cost of individuality.

Conformity, conversely, serves as the scaffolding upon which society erects its structure of order and stability. It seeks to create a framework that fosters cohesion, predictability, and a sense of security. Conformity is the glue that binds communities together, offering a common ground upon which shared goals can be constructed. At its core, it functions as a vital social contract, establishing norms and expectations that guide our interactions and define our roles.

Yet, in its unrestrained form, conformity may exert a chilling influence on innovation and the pursuit of individuality. When conformity hardens into an unquestioned rule, it has the potential to silence dissenting voices, quell the flames of creativity, and cast a shadow over unconventional ideas. Some of the most transformative concepts and movements have emerged from the margins of convention, highlighting the delicate balance required to harness conformity effectively.

As we navigate this intricate dance between community and conformity, we must rely on wisdom, discernment, and a deep well of empathy. It calls upon us to recognize when our sense of belonging begins to smother the individuality of our members, or when our conformity threatens to snuff out the life force of innovation. Achieving this delicate equilibrium demands a finely tuned awareness of the dynamics at play.

True strength emerges when these two forces find harmony in their interaction. A vibrant and healthy community does not suppress individuality; rather, it celebrates the unique contributions of its members. It acknowledges that the richness of the collective arises from the diverse colors and textures that each individual brings to the tapestry. Similarly, when approached with nuance and adaptability, conformity can serve as a framework for cooperation without stifling the sparks of innovation that often arise from the fringes of convention.

In our pursuit of this elusive equilibrium, we must be prepared to challenge entrenched norms that no longer serve the greater good. We must cultivate empathy and open-mindedness, creating an environment where both individuality and shared purpose can coexist and flourish. This is a tightrope walk, a nuanced balancing act that, when mastered, allows us to build communities that thrive on the brilliance of their diverse members while upholding the common values that bind us together.

Resisting the confines of a false dichotomy that forces us to choose between community and conformity, we strive for a harmonious union. In such a union, community and conformity coexist in a dynamic partnership, creating an environment where individuality and shared purpose not only coexist but also mutually enrich and elevate one another. This, indeed, is the essence of our collective existence—a symphony of diversity and unity that resonates with the profound beauty of the human experience.

In our quest for this delicate equilibrium, we must acknowledge that it is not a static destination but a dynamic journey. It requires continuous reflection, adaptability, and a willingness to evolve as circumstances change. The interplay of community and conformity is a living narrative in which each generation must play its part, learning from the past while forging a path toward a future where the potential for human flourishing knows no bounds.

Furthermore, the balance between community and conformity extends beyond the microcosms of individual societies and communities. It is a global consideration, where diverse cultures and nations must find ways to harmonize their collective identities while respecting the individuality of their constituents. In the interconnected world of the 21st century, this balance is not only a matter of social cohesion but also a foundation for global peace and progress.

As we navigate this intricate dance, we must be mindful of the power dynamics at play. The forces of conformity can sometimes be wielded by those in positions of authority to maintain control and suppress dissent. In such instances, the preservation of individuality and the defense of diverse voices become vital tools in the fight for justice and equality.

Moreover, technology and the digital age have introduced new dimensions to the community-conformity dialectic. Social media platforms and online communities offer unprecedented opportunities for individuals to connect and express their unique identities. However, they also present challenges, as they can amplify conformity pressures through algorithms that encourage conformity to prevailing opinions.

The art of achieving a balanced relationship between community and conformity also extends to education. Educational institutions have the responsibility to foster both a sense of belonging within communities and the cultivation of independent critical thinking. Striking this balance is essential for preparing future generations to navigate an increasingly complex and interconnected world.

In conclusion, the delicate equilibrium between community and conformity is a theme that runs deep in the human experience. It touches upon our need for belonging, our yearning for individuality, and our quest for a harmonious coexistence. To harness the potential of this equilibrium is to embark on a journey of self-discovery and collective progress, one that challenges us to recognize the power and pitfalls of both community and conformity.

As we chart our course through this intricate dance, let us remain vigilant, compassionate, and open to change. Let us embrace the richness of diversity within our communities while upholding the values that unite us. Let us continue to evolve, as individuals and societies, in our understanding of this intricate interplay, so that we may navigate it with grace and wisdom, crafting a future where both our collective identity and our individuality thrive in harmonious balance.

CHAPTER THIRTY-SIX

Beyond Appearances: True Inclusivity in Action

In the ongoing quest for a more inclusive society, we find ourselves engaged in a compelling and multifaceted struggle—a battle that revolves around the critical distinction between authentic inclusivity and its deceptive counterpart, often termed tokenism. At its core, this battle revolves around the noble pursuit of embracing diversity, creating spaces where voices from all walks of life are genuinely welcomed, valued, and heard. It is the embodiment of true inclusivity, a goal that aligns with the core principles of human equality and dignity.

Yet, amidst the pursuit of inclusivity's virtuous ideals, a shadowy figure emerges—tokenism. This elusive concept masquerades as inclusivity but, in reality, perpetuates the status quo while displaying a superficial façade of diversity. Tokenism involves including a single individual from a marginalized group, often reducing them to a symbolic token—a representative figurehead. Although this may appear well-intentioned, beneath the surface lies a darker truth: the exploitation of diversity to maintain appearances.

Inclusivity, the virtuous aspect of this dual nature, signifies a profound commitment to constructing spaces where everyone genuinely belongs. It requires actively seeking diverse perspectives, recognizing the inherent value of individuals regardless of their backgrounds, and celebrating the tapestry of diversity that enriches our society. Inclusivity embodies a genuine celebration of differences, symbolizing our collective growth and progress as a human community.

In contrast, tokenism, the sinister twin, reduces diversity to a mere checkbox on a bureaucratic to-do list. It manifests in the selection of a conference speaker based solely on their demographic attributes or the employment of an individual to fulfill a diversity quota, devoid of true consideration for their talents and potential. Tokenism is a superficial gesture that serves as a shield against accusations of discrimination while failing to address the deep-seated, systemic issues that fuel inequality.

The crux of the matter resides in the intent and approach. Inclusivity is rooted in a sincere desire to effect meaningful change. It involves dismantling the barriers that divide us, actively listening to marginalized voices, and confronting the biased systems that perpetuate discrimination. Inclusivity demands effort, empathy, and an unwavering commitment to transformation. Tokenism, on the other hand, is driven by optics, a desire to maintain the status quo, and an aversion to confronting the deeper, systemic issues at play.

As we continue our journey toward a more inclusive world, it is imperative to remain vigilant and consistently evaluate our motives and methods. True inclusivity requires dedication, an unwavering commitment to breaking down the walls that divide us, and a willingness to acknowledge the inherent worth of every individual, regardless of their background. It is a dynamic process, a perpetual journey rather than a finite destination. Tokenism, in stark contrast, is a shortcut that ultimately leads to stagnation—a mere illusion of progress.

The choice between inclusivity and tokenism is a reflection of our values and priorities as individuals and as a society. Our collective aspiration should be to foster a world where inclusivity is not just a buzzword or a superficial veneer but a lived reality—a world where we recognize and celebrate the intrinsic worth of every person, irrespective of their background. Such a world represents not only an aspiration but a profound commitment to justice, equality, and the betterment of humanity as a whole.

In this ongoing struggle, let us not be swayed by the allure of tokenism's deceptive simplicity but instead be inspired by the richness and depth that authentic inclusivity brings to our lives. Let us strive for inclusivity that transcends mere appearances and becomes a fundamental cornerstone of our societies—a beacon of hope, a testament to our commitment to the principles of diversity, equity, and inclusion.

Authentic inclusivity entails not only inviting marginalized voices to the table but also actively listening to their experiences, concerns, and perspectives. It requires an ongoing dialogue and a commitment to addressing the root causes of inequality. Inclusivity is not a one-time action; it is a continuous and evolving process that demands introspection, education, and a willingness to evolve.

Tokenism, by contrast, represents a shallow and short-sighted approach. It seeks to meet diversity quotas and check boxes without delving into the substantive issues of discrimination and inequality. Tokenism often leads to the marginalization of the very individuals it purports to represent, as they may feel pressure to conform to preconceived notions or act as spokespersons for their entire group.

Inclusivity, as a guiding principle, challenges us to examine the power structures that perpetuate inequality. It prompts us to confront biases and prejudices, both overt and subtle, and to dismantle systems that disadvantage certain groups. Inclusivity recognizes that creating a level playing field requires a concerted effort to address historical and systemic injustices.

On the other hand, tokenism often serves as a convenient way to avoid confronting these deeper issues. It can give the appearance of progress while maintaining the status quo. Tokenism can be used as a shield against accusations of discrimination, deflecting attention away from the need for systemic change.

In our journey toward authentic inclusivity, it is essential to remain committed to the long-term goal of creating a more equitable and just society. This requires not only inviting diverse voices into spaces of influence but also actively working to ensure that their perspectives are valued and integrated into decision-making processes.

Inclusivity is not about simply ticking boxes or meeting quotas. It is about recognizing the value of diversity and actively seeking out voices that have historically been marginalized or silenced. It is about creating an environment where individuals from all backgrounds can thrive, contribute, and lead.

In conclusion, the battle between authentic inclusivity and tokenism is a crucial one in our ongoing quest for a more just and equitable world. It challenges us to examine our motives and methods and to strive for meaningful and lasting change. Let us choose the path of authentic inclusivity, where every individual is valued for their unique contributions, and where diversity is celebrated not as a mere checkbox but as a source of strength and richness in our societies.

CHAPTER THIRTY-SEVEN

Mirrored Paradox: Navigating Self-Reflection and Self-Obsession

In the vast theater of self-exploration, where the intricacies of our inner world are laid bare, two contrasting actors often take center stage: Self-Reflection and Self-Obsession. These players, both donning the masks of introspection, stand before the mirror of self-awareness, yet their intentions and outcomes could not be more divergent.

On one hand, Self-Reflection emerges as the virtuous scholar of the self. With humility as its guiding light, it approaches the mirror of introspection seeking to understand, learn, and evolve. It recognizes its flaws and virtues alike, embracing them as stepping stones on the path to growth and self-improvement. Self-Reflection casts a wide net, inviting insights from others and harnessing the profound power of introspection to illuminate the recesses of the soul. Its purpose is enlightenment, and its script is one of profound self-discovery.

In stark contrast, Self-Obsession assumes the role of the cunning trickster of the mind. It, too, gazes into the mirror, but its focus is myopic, fixated solely on its own reflection. It adores its virtues while willfully blinding itself to its flaws. Self-Obsession harbors no interest in growth; instead, it craves validation, perpetually seeking approval and admiration from the audience. Its script is a soliloquy of ego, and it can often be deaf to the voices and perspectives of others.

The paradox emerges when we consider the hidden agendas of these two actors. Self-Reflection, though inherently virtuous, can sometimes employ a flawed approach. It may lead to self-criticism that spirals into debilitating self-doubt, or it could foster excessive introspection, paralyzing action with endless contemplation. In its pursuit of self-improvement, it may even, at times, verge on self-absorption when the quest for perfection becomes an all-consuming obsession.

On the other hand, Self-Obsession, while intrinsically flawed, may occasionally house a flicker of good intention. It can fuel determination and ambition, propelling individuals to achieve remarkable feats driven by the insatiable desire for recognition. It might also serve as a temporary shield against self-doubt in the face of adversity, providing a necessary boost of confidence.

The mirror's paradox beckons us to navigate the labyrinthine corridors of self-awareness, striving to find a harmonious balance between these two dramatic actors. We must learn to engage in self-reflection without succumbing to the siren call of self-obsession. To do so, we must acknowledge our flaws with kindness, embracing them as opportunities for growth rather than sources of shame. We should seek validation from within, cultivating a robust internal compass that guides us through the tumultuous waters of life. Moreover, we must invite diverse perspectives into our narrative, enriching our self-awareness and broadening our understanding of the world.

In the grand drama of life, we are not mere spectators but active participants, the directors of our self-reflection and the playwrights of our self-obsession. The key to a fulfilling narrative lies in crafting a story where self-awareness takes center stage as the protagonist, humility serves as the guiding light, and growth emerges as the ultimate climax. For it is in the delicate interplay of these contrasting forces that we unearth the true essence of our ever-evolving selves.

In the theater of self-exploration, the mirror reflects not only our image but the multifaceted drama of our existence, inviting us to embrace the complexity within and strive for a symphony of self-awareness that resonates with authenticity and purpose.

Self-Reflection, like an astute detective, navigates the intricate web of our thoughts, emotions, and experiences. It seeks to uncover the hidden gems of self-knowledge, shining a light on the corners of our psyche we may have otherwise left unexplored. This process of self-inquiry allows us to make conscious choices, to grow, and to align our actions with our values.

Self-Obsession, however, is akin to a self-absorbed actor who steals the spotlight from the ensemble. It becomes so engrossed in its own narrative that it loses touch with the broader stage of life. It measures its worth solely by external validation and applause, often neglecting the deeper, quieter, and more authentic aspects of the self.

The challenge, then, is to strike a harmonious balance between these two forces. Self-Reflection should be our guiding star, illuminating our path with wisdom and self-awareness. It can help us recognize our strengths and weaknesses, fostering empathy not only for ourselves but also for others. However, we must be vigilant against its potential pitfalls—excessive self-criticism, self-doubt, or the paralysis of over-analysis.

Conversely, Self-Obsession should be harnessed as a fleeting ally, not a relentless adversary. It can ignite our passion and determination, driving us to achieve remarkable feats. But we must keep it in check, preventing it from transforming into a destructive ego that blinds us to our flaws and distances us from genuine connection with others.

The mirror of self-awareness is not static; it is a dynamic, ever-evolving reflection of our inner world. Like skilled actors, we must adapt our roles as the script of life unfolds. We must recognize that self-awareness is not a destination but a journey—a continual exploration of the self's depths and dimensions.

Moreover, we must cultivate the art of self-compassion. Just as we offer understanding and forgiveness to others, we should extend the same kindness to ourselves. Self-Reflection can be a compassionate friend, helping us embrace our imperfections as part of our human experience. Self-Obsession can be tempered with self-love, guiding us to seek validation from within, rather than relying solely on external praise.

In conclusion, the paradox of self-reflection and self-obsession is a timeless theme in the theater of human existence. It challenges us to craft a narrative where self-awareness takes the lead, humility guides our actions, and growth emerges as the ultimate masterpiece. As we tread the boards of self-discovery, let us strive for the sublime balance between these contrasting actors, allowing self-awareness to be our compass, humility our beacon, and growth our eternal pursuit. In this ongoing drama of life, we have the power to shape our narrative and, in doing so, uncover the profound truths that lie within our ever-evolving selves.

CHAPTER THIRTY-EIGHT

Path to Peace: Navigating Reconciliation and Escalation

In the turbulent seas of conflict, the choices we make can chart a course either toward reconciliation or escalation. It's a daunting crossroads where morality is entwined with pragmatism, and where the distinction between right and wrong isn't always clear-cut.

Reconciliation, on one hand, stands as a beacon of hope, promising healing and harmony. It embodies the ideals of forgiveness and understanding, seeking common ground in the face of discord. Yet, reconciliation can sometimes bear the weight of impracticality. In its unwavering pursuit of peace, it may inadvertently enable injustice or perpetuate suffering.

On the other side of the spectrum, we find escalation. Often seen as the antithesis of reconciliation, it can be a response to aggression, a defense against perceived threats. But herein lies the paradox: Escalation, though rooted in self-preservation, can unleash chaos and destruction. Its path, strewn with casualties, raises the specter of "fighting fire with fire."

So, is there a middle ground? Can we conceive a path where reconciliation's goodness of heart meets escalation's duty to protect? Can we negotiate peace without compromising justice?

Perhaps therein lies the challenge and the solution: a nuanced approach that acknowledges the merits of both sides. Reconciliation's compassion and understanding can pave the way for dialogue, while escalation's vigilance can safeguard against exploitation. In this dynamic interplay, we may uncover a path that respects the past, ensures accountability, and cultivates a future where the good intentions of both sides can flourish.

In the end, it's not about choosing one over the other; it's about recognizing that the quest for peace is often a balancing act. The true test of wisdom lies in navigating this delicate equilibrium—a path where reconciliation and escalation, despite their inherent contradictions, can coexist, ultimately leading us to a world where the good agenda of peace prevails over the bad approach of conflict.

Navigating the treacherous waters of conflict is akin to sailing through a stormy sea, where every decision carries profound consequences. Reconciliation, with its call for empathy and dialogue, represents the noble aspiration of healing rifts and fostering understanding. It beckons us to extend the olive branch, to bridge divides that have festered for generations. Yet, it is not without its challenges.

Reconciliation often faces criticism for its perceived impracticality, especially when dealing with deeply entrenched conflicts fueled by historical grievances. Critics argue that pursuing reconciliation at any cost may inadvertently allow perpetrators of injustice to escape accountability. This raises the question: can reconciliation truly be achieved without compromising justice?

On the opposite end of the spectrum stands escalation—a response driven by self-preservation and the instinct to protect one's interests. It is often seen as a necessary defense mechanism in the face of aggression or looming threats. However, the paradox lies in the fact that escalation, while initially rooted in the pursuit of security, can spiral into a cycle of violence and chaos. The age-old adage of "fighting fire with fire" resonates here, reminding us of the risks associated with a purely aggressive approach to conflict.

So, where does the answer lie? Is there a way to harmonize the heart's desire for reconciliation with the mind's instinct for self-preservation? Can we craft a path that respects the principles of both sides, without sacrificing justice?

The challenge before us is to navigate this complex terrain with nuance and wisdom. It involves recognizing that the quest for peace is not a binary choice between reconciliation and escalation but a delicate dance where both can coexist. Reconciliation can set the stage for dialogue, while escalation can act as a safeguard against exploitation. In this intricate interplay, we may discover a path that acknowledges historical wrongs, ensures accountability for past actions, and paves the way for a future where the benevolent intentions of both sides can flourish.

In essence, it's about striking a balance, for wisdom often resides in equilibrium. It's about crafting a path where reconciliation and escalation, despite their apparent contradictions, complement each other, ultimately leading us to a world where the pursuit of peace transcends the approach of conflict.

At the heart of this complex issue is the recognition that there is no one-size-fits-all solution. Each conflict is unique, shaped by its historical, cultural, and political context. What works in one situation may not work in another. Hence, flexibility and adaptability are key in navigating these tumultuous waters.

Moreover, the role of mediators and diplomats in conflict resolution cannot be understated. They are tasked with the delicate mission of finding common ground while upholding principles of justice. Their skill lies in striking a balance that allows reconciliation to flourish without sacrificing the need for accountability.

In conclusion, the dichotomy between reconciliation and escalation in the face of conflict reflects the intricate nature of human interactions. It challenges us to find a middle path, one that respects the ideals of both sides while recognizing the practicalities of the situation. It reminds us that the pursuit of peace is an art that requires wisdom, patience, and a deep understanding of the complexities at play. In our quest for harmony, let us strive to chart a course that honors the best of both worlds—a path where reconciliation and escalation coexist, leading us toward a future where the winds of peace prevail over the storm of conflict.

The importance of communication cannot be overstated in the realm of conflict resolution. Reconciliation often hinges on the ability to open channels of dialogue, allowing parties to voice their grievances and seek common ground. Effective communication can bridge chasms of misunderstanding and mistrust, fostering an environment where reconciliation becomes possible.

However, communication alone may not suffice. Escalation, driven by the need to protect one's interests, sometimes necessitates a readiness to defend oneself. In such cases, the challenge lies in tempering escalation with the knowledge that a solely combative approach can lead to a self-perpetuating cycle of violence.

The role of leadership is paramount in navigating these complex waters. Leaders must possess the wisdom to discern when reconciliation is feasible and when escalation is unavoidable. They must be adept at balancing the virtues of peace with the imperatives of security, ensuring that neither side's legitimate concerns are dismissed.

In certain conflicts, transitional justice mechanisms can play a vital role. These mechanisms seek to address past atrocities and provide a framework for accountability and healing. By acknowledging historical wrongs and holding perpetrators accountable, they can pave the way for reconciliation without sacrificing justice.

Furthermore, it's essential to involve civil society and grassroots initiatives in the process of conflict resolution. These actors often have a deep understanding of the local context and can contribute innovative solutions that might not be apparent to external parties.

The power of education should not be underestimated in the quest for reconciliation. By promoting a culture of tolerance and understanding, educational institutions can foster the values necessary for peaceful coexistence. Moreover, they can help challenge the narratives of hatred and division that often fuel conflicts.

Ultimately, the path to reconciliation and the threshold for escalation are contingent on the specifics of each conflict. There is no one-size-fits-all formula. What remains constant, however, is the need for a thoughtful, nuanced approach that weighs the values of peace and justice against the exigencies of the situation.

In conclusion, the dichotomy between reconciliation and escalation presents a profound challenge in the realm of conflict resolution. It calls upon our wisdom, adaptability, and empathy to find a path that respects both the pursuit of peace and the call for justice. It reminds us that there are no easy answers, but by navigating these complexities with a commitment to dialogue, understanding, and accountability, we can aspire to a world where conflicts are resolved with compassion and reason, and where the seas of turmoil are navigated toward the shores of lasting peace.

CHAPTER THIRTY-NINE

Thin Line: Balancing Security and Surveillance

In the modern world, the need for security is undeniable. We yearn for safe homes, secure finances, and protected nations. It's only natural to seek the shield of security against the uncertainties of life. But what happens when the very guardians of security cross a precarious threshold, morphing into invasive sentinels of surveillance?

On one hand, we have "security," a concept draped in the comforting cloak of safeguarding our well-being. It stands as the guardian of order, defending us against threats, both seen and unseen. It's the promise of a peaceful night's sleep and the assurance that our privacy remains intact. Security is, indeed, a noble aspect of our existence.

However, on the other hand, we confront "surveillance," a shadowy figure lurking at the edges of our lives. While it may be a necessary tool in maintaining order and preventing harm, it wields a double-edged sword. Surveillance can start with good intentions—a desire to protect—but it can swiftly devolve into an insatiable appetite for control. It may argue for national security but creep into the territory of infringement on personal liberties.

In this juxtaposition, we find ourselves at a crossroads. We must balance our yearning for security with a vigilant watch over the encroachment of surveillance. It is a delicate dance, akin to taming a wild beast while ensuring it doesn't devour the very essence of our freedom and privacy.

The challenge is clear: How do we uphold the principles of security without succumbing to the allure of surveillance's all-seeing eye? Can we find a path that safeguards our well-being without trampling on the sacred ground of individual liberty?

These questions do not offer simple answers. They beckon us to tread thoughtfully, to engage in meaningful discourse, and to hold those in power accountable. The duality of security versus surveillance is a reminder that even the noblest of intentions can lead down treacherous paths. It urges us to strike a balance, to redefine the boundaries, and to ensure that our quest for security does not inadvertently become a march toward oppression.

As we navigate this thin line between security and surveillance, we must remember that our actions today shape the world we inherit tomorrow. It is a journey fraught with complexity, but it is one we must embark upon with open eyes and vigilant hearts.

To fully appreciate the gravity of this dilemma, we must first acknowledge that security and surveillance are not binary states. They exist on a spectrum, with nuances and shades that demand our careful consideration. Security, when wielded with wisdom, serves as a shield against external threats. It can bring peace to troubled lands and protect individuals from harm. In essence, it fosters an environment where our rights and freedoms can flourish.

Yet, surveillance, when left unchecked, can morph into a tool of oppression. It can erode the very liberties we hold dear, casting a pervasive net that monitors our every move, both online and offline. The potential for abuse is vast, with the erosion of privacy and the stifling of dissent being just some of the pernicious consequences.

To navigate this complex terrain, we must prioritize transparency and accountability in the systems of surveillance. It is incumbent upon governments and institutions to establish clear guidelines, checks, and balances to prevent the misuse of surveillance powers. Oversight by independent bodies and a robust legal framework are essential to ensure that surveillance remains a tool for protecting society, not controlling it.

Furthermore, we must engage in a broader societal dialogue about the boundaries of surveillance. What level of intrusion are we willing to tolerate in the name of security? How do we strike a balance between protecting individual rights and safeguarding collective interests? These are questions that require open debate and consensus-building.

As individuals, we also bear responsibility in this equation. We must be vigilant about protecting our privacy and advocating for our rights. This entails being mindful of the data we share online, understanding the implications of new technologies, and supporting organizations that champion digital rights.

In conclusion, the interplay between security and surveillance is one of the defining challenges of our time. It forces us to confront the complexities of modern life, where the pursuit of safety can sometimes encroach upon the preservation of liberty. Our ability to strike a delicate balance between these two vital aspects of our society will determine the nature of the world we pass on to future generations. It is a journey that demands constant vigilance, ethical introspection, and a commitment to the principles that underpin a just and free society.

In examining this dichotomy, we must also consider the rapid advancements in technology. The digital age has brought forth tools that have made both security and surveillance more potent and pervasive. While these technologies have undoubtedly enhanced our ability to protect against threats, they have also opened the door to unprecedented levels of intrusion.

The ubiquitous presence of cameras, both in public spaces and in our personal devices, highlights the omnipresence of surveillance in our daily lives. Data is constantly collected, processed, and analyzed, often without our knowledge or consent. Our online activities, once private, are subject to scrutiny by both government agencies and private corporations.

This digital era has given rise to concerns about the erosion of privacy. The very fabric of our personal lives, our thoughts, desires, and behaviors, is laid bare in the digital realm. It's a realm where the boundaries between security and surveillance blur, where the promise of convenience and connectivity is juxtaposed with the potential for abuse and intrusion.

As we grapple with these challenges, it becomes apparent that the protection of individual rights and freedoms is paramount. We must ensure that the power of surveillance is wielded judiciously and with strict adherence to legal and ethical boundaries. It is imperative that we enact legislation and establish safeguards that protect the privacy of citizens in the digital age.

Moreover, we must foster a culture of transparency and accountability. Citizens should have access to information about how their data is collected and used, and they should have the means to challenge any misuse or abuse of surveillance powers. This requires a partnership between governments, technology companies, and civil society to establish guidelines and practices that strike a balance between security and individual liberty.

In the midst of this ongoing debate, we must also remember that the boundaries of security and surveillance are not static. They evolve in response to changing threats, technologies, and societal norms. Therefore, our approach to this delicate balance must remain flexible and adaptable. We must be willing to reassess and recalibrate as circumstances change to ensure that our rights and freedoms are safeguarded.

In conclusion, the tension between security and surveillance is a defining challenge of our times, one that transcends national borders and touches the lives of individuals around the world. It is a challenge that demands our unwavering commitment to the principles of freedom and justice. As we navigate this complex landscape, we must be vigilant, proactive, and mindful of the potential consequences of our choices. Only through a thoughtful and balanced approach can we hope to strike the right equilibrium between the need for security and the protection of individual liberties.

CHAPTER FORTY

Guidance Unbound: Navigating Parental Care and Overprotection

In the intricate dance of parenting, one of the most delicate steps involves finding the right balance between guidance and protection. On one side of the stage stands "Parental Guidance," a role that aims to empower children, providing them with the tools to navigate life's twists and turns independently. On the other side, we have "Overprotection," a well-intentioned but potentially stifling role that seeks to shield children from harm at any cost.

Parental guidance is the virtuous advocate of growth and resilience. It encourages children to explore, to make choices, and to learn from their experiences. It is the gentle nudge that says, "You can do it; I believe in you." It fosters self-confidence, independence, and a sense of responsibility.

On the contrary, overprotection, while rooted in love and concern, can inadvertently cast a shadow over a child's development. It's the voice that says, "I'll handle it for you." It shields children from adversity, but in doing so, it may also shield them from the invaluable lessons adversity can bring. It can nurture dependence rather than independence, fear rather than courage.

However, it is essential to recognize that the intent behind overprotection often comes from a place of profound care. Parents who overprotect may have witnessed life's hardships firsthand and wish to spare their children similar pain. They envision a world where their child remains unscathed by the harshness of reality.

It's a noble agenda, indeed, but it inadvertently risks stifling the very growth and resilience that children need to thrive. In this intricate dance, the challenge lies in finding the harmony between protecting and guiding—where love meets wisdom.

So, how can we embrace the virtuous aspects of both roles while avoiding their pitfalls? Perhaps it begins with open communication and trust. Parents can guide their children through life's challenges while allowing them the space to learn from both success and failure. It's about instilling values, imparting skills, and then letting them take their own steps, knowing they have a safety net of support when needed.

In the end, the delicate balance between parental guidance and overprotection can be a lifelong journey—one where both parents and children learn and adapt together. It's a dance where the steps may falter at times, but the rhythm of love and shared experiences ultimately guides the way.

Navigating this dance requires recognizing that children are not merely vessels to be protected but individuals who need the freedom to discover their own strengths and weaknesses. By guiding rather than dictating, parents can empower their children to make informed decisions and learn from the consequences, both positive and negative. This approach builds resilience and self-reliance, qualities that will serve them well throughout life.

At the same time, parents must be mindful of their own fears and anxieties. Overprotection often arises from a desire to shield children from harm, but it can inadvertently convey a lack of trust in their abilities. Parents can work on managing their anxieties and fostering an environment where children feel safe discussing their experiences and seeking guidance when needed.

The journey of parenting is fraught with uncertainties, and the balance between guidance and protection is a nuanced one. It's about recognizing that children need room to grow and make mistakes, but they also need a loving and supportive presence to help them navigate life's challenges. It's a constant evolution, as children grow and face new stages of development.

As children mature, the role of parental guidance evolves as well. It shifts from providing direct solutions to offering guidance through discussions and shared decision-making. This transition allows children to develop their problem-solving skills and gain a sense of ownership over their choices.

Ultimately, the dance of parenting is a lifelong commitment. It's about being there for your children, not only to shield them from harm but also to empower them to become resilient, independent, and responsible individuals. It's about finding the harmony between guidance and protection, adjusting the steps as needed, and celebrating the beauty of growth and self-discovery along the way.

In this dance, both parents and children play their parts, learning and adapting together. It's a journey marked by love, trust, and the unwavering belief that, with the right balance of guidance and protection, children can flourish and become the best versions of themselves.

The essence of parental guidance lies in fostering a sense of autonomy in children. It is about offering them the tools, knowledge, and emotional support they need to make informed decisions and face life's challenges head-on. This approach encourages self-reliance, critical thinking, and the development of problem-solving skills.

On the other hand, overprotection, despite its well-intentioned nature, can inadvertently communicate to children that they are incapable of handling difficulties on their own. This message can undermine their self-esteem and hinder their ability to cope with adversity when they inevitably encounter it. In essence, overprotection may shield children from short-term discomfort but deprive them of the long-term growth and resilience that result from overcoming challenges.

The delicate balance between these roles often requires parents to assess their motivations and fears. It's crucial to recognize when the desire to protect arises from one's own anxieties rather than the child's well-being. By addressing these fears and anxieties, parents can better navigate the terrain between guidance and protection, allowing their children the space to flourish while providing a safety net when needed.

Additionally, parents can foster independence by encouraging children to take on age-appropriate responsibilities and make choices within set boundaries. This gradual release of control allows children to develop a sense of agency and responsibility over time. It's a process that acknowledges their growth and readiness to take on more significant challenges.

Furthermore, parents can model resilience and problem-solving skills in their own lives, showing their children that setbacks and failures are opportunities for growth and learning. By embracing these principles themselves, parents can lead by example and inspire their children to face adversity with courage and determination.

In summary, the intricate dance of parenting involves finding a delicate balance between guidance and protection. Parental guidance empowers children to develop independence and resilience, while overprotection, though well-intentioned, can inadvertently hinder their growth. Striking this balance requires open communication, trust, and self-awareness on the part of parents. It's a lifelong journey where parents learn alongside their children, fostering self-reliance, critical thinking, and a strong sense of self-worth. In the end, the dance of parenting is a beautiful journey of growth and development for both parents and children, marked by love, trust, and the shared goal of nurturing resilient and independent individuals.

CHAPTER FORTY-ONE

Winds of Change: Navigating Civic Engagement and Agitation

In the grand theater of societal evolution, there are two key players: Civic Engagement and Agitation. Both are driven by a shared desire for change, but they adopt vastly different scripts and stages. These contrasting forces are the very heartbeat of a society in flux, shaping its destiny.

Civic Engagement, the responsible and diligent protagonist in this social drama, takes center stage as the embodiment of order and structure. It is the art of participating constructively within the established systems and norms of society. Civic engagement is the ballot cast in a democratic election, a quiet but powerful voice advocating for change through peaceful protest, and the selfless volunteer at a local charity, silently working to alleviate suffering. It stands on the moral high ground of legitimacy, championing the rule of law and adherence to established procedures.

Agitation, on the other hand, emerges as the audacious and untamed antagonist in this narrative. It defies the conventions of patience and gradual change, refusing to wait for transformation to come of its own accord. Agitation manifests as street protests echoing with chants of justice, acts of civil disobedience that challenge oppressive systems, and voices of dissent that ring out unapologetically. It confronts the status quo head-on, demanding change with urgency and vigor.

In this perpetual clash of ideologies, we encounter a profound paradox. Civic engagement is often applauded for its inherent "goodness" as it upholds order, legality, and civility. However, it can sometimes become mired in complacency, stagnant in the face of pressing issues, or even unwittingly complicit in perpetuating unjust systems. The veneer of its "good" approach may, at times, obscure its lack of urgency or its failure to enact real change.

Conversely, Agitation often finds itself draped in the garb of "badness" due to its disruptive, confrontational, and often chaotic nature. Yet, beneath the surface, it is driven by a deep-seated desire to confront wrongs, dismantle oppressive structures, and exact justice. Its "bad" approach is frequently rooted in a profound commitment to righting society's gravest injustices.

In truth, both Civic Engagement and Agitation possess crucial roles within the grand narrative of social progress. Separating them is not an option, for one without the other can lead to either stagnation or anarchic chaos. They are the Yin and Yang, the dual forces that propel societal transformation forward.

The challenge does not lie in choosing one over the other, but rather in recognizing when and how each is needed. Civic Engagement lays the groundwork for lasting change, its steady hand constructing the foundation upon which society can build a better future. Agitation, in contrast, often serves as the compelling driving force when the very foundations crack under the weight of injustice, forcing society to confront its demons.

As we contemplate the delicate dance between Civic Engagement and Agitation, let us acknowledge that the path to a more just and equitable world is often a meandering one. It is a path illuminated by both the measured steps of Civic Engagement and the fiery leaps of Agitation. It is not a matter of discarding one in favor of the other but rather embracing the intricate complexities of both as we navigate the turbulent waters of societal change.

In the end, it is the interplay between these two forces that keeps society evolving and progressing. They are the dialectic tension that sparks conversations, reforms institutions, and ultimately reshapes the destiny of nations. The grand theater of societal evolution is a stage where both Civic Engagement and Agitation have their rightful roles, each contributing to the unfolding drama that shapes the course of history.

Civic Engagement, as the embodiment of order and stability, provides the continuity that allows societies to function smoothly. It is the engine that drives the incremental changes necessary for long-term progress. When individuals engage civically, they vote for leaders who represent their values, they participate in community initiatives, and they seek to reform systems from within. Civic Engagement is often characterized by patience, dialogue, and the pursuit of incremental reforms.

Agitation, on the other hand, serves as a necessary disruptor. It is the force that challenges the status quo when it becomes entrenched in injustice or inequality. Agitation arises when there is a sense of urgency, a need for immediate change. It is fueled by passion, courage, and the refusal to accept the injustices of the world. Historically, movements like the civil rights movement, women's suffrage, and labor rights have been driven by Agitation.

In the ongoing dialogue between these two forces, there is a delicate balance to be struck. An overemphasis on Civic Engagement alone can lead to complacency and a reluctance to challenge deeply rooted injustices. Conversely, an overreliance on Agitation can result in chaos and the erosion of societal norms and stability.

The optimal approach, it seems, is a dynamic one that recognizes the strengths of both Civic Engagement and Agitation. In the face of systemic issues that demand change, Civic Engagement can provide the groundwork for sustainable solutions. It can offer a platform for dialogue, consensus-building, and the implementation of reforms. It is the patient gardener tending to the roots of a tree, ensuring its long-term growth.

However, when the existing structures prove resistant to change or when there is an urgent need to address a crisis, Agitation steps in to break the status quo. It shakes the foundations, demanding immediate attention and action. It is the firefighter rushing into a burning building to save lives, regardless of the rules.

In reality, these two forces are not mutually exclusive. They often overlap and complement each other. Civic Engagement can be a precursor to Agitation, as individuals and groups engage with established systems but find their efforts stonewalled. Likewise, Agitation can lead to Civic Engagement when protest movements transition into advocacy for legislative change.

Ultimately, the effectiveness of these forces depends on context and timing. Society must remain flexible enough to adapt to changing circumstances, knowing when to lean on the stability of Civic Engagement and when to harness the urgency of Agitation.

In conclusion, the interplay between Civic Engagement and Agitation is the heartbeat of societal progress. Both are essential to the evolution of a just and equitable society. It is in recognizing the strengths and limitations of each that we can navigate the complex terrain of change with wisdom and effectiveness. As we continue to strive for a better world, let us remember that it is the harmonious dance between these two forces that propels us forward on the path of social transformation.

CHAPTER FORTY-TWO

Dilemma of Progress: Economic Growth versus Exploitation

In the grand theater of societal evolution, there are two key players: Economic growth, the elixir of modern societies, promises prosperity, progress, and a better quality of life for all. It is the guiding star of nations, the beacon of hope for developing countries, and the yardstick of success for governments. Yet, as we bask in the glow of growth charts and rising GDP figures, a nagging shadow looms large - the specter of exploitation.

One aspect of this equation champions economic growth as the path to advancement. It argues that growth brings jobs, increases incomes, and raises living standards. It fuels innovation, funds social programs, and creates opportunities for education and healthcare. Indeed, growth is heralded as the engine that drives nations forward, uplifting millions from poverty and igniting the flame of progress.

But here's the rub. Economic growth often strides forward with a heavy tread, leaving behind a trail of exploitation in its wake. The pursuit of profit can sometimes turn blind eyes to the plight of workers toiling in unsafe conditions for meager wages. It can disregard environmental concerns, leaving ecosystems devastated in the relentless march toward development. It can foster income inequality, where the rich get richer, and the poor struggle to make ends meet. In its unbridled form, growth can perpetuate social injustices and undermine the very ideals it claims to champion.

On the other side of this equation, we find the specter of exploitation reluctantly shouldering a noble agenda. This aspect recognizes the dark underbelly of growth and calls for justice. It argues that we must not exploit human labor, degrade our environment, or trample over marginalized communities in the name of progress. It calls for ethical business practices, fair wages, and sustainable development that respects the planet's finite resources.

Yet, exploitation, too, has its moral dilemma. It often wields the sword of resistance and protest, sometimes undermining economic growth altogether. It can stifle innovation, discourage entrepreneurship, and deter investment. In its zealous pursuit of justice, it may inadvertently hold back the very progress it seeks to rectify.

So, where does the balance lie in this age-old struggle between economic growth and exploitation? It's a question that policymakers grapple with, and one that each of us, as members of society, must confront. Can we have the best of both worlds - a robust economy that lifts all boats, and a just society that doesn't leave anyone behind? Or must we forever navigate the rocky terrain, attempting to find a compromise that eludes easy definition?

The answer, it seems, lies in our collective will to shape the narrative. Economic growth is a powerful force, but it's not inherently virtuous. Exploitation is a formidable adversary, but it's not a flawless champion of justice. It is up to us, as individuals and as a society, to demand a balance that nurtures prosperity while safeguarding human dignity and the planet we call home.

The dilemma of progress persists, and the conversation endures. In this ongoing discourse, may we find the wisdom to forge a path that bridges the gap between growth and justice, for the benefit of all humankind.

As we navigate this intricate dance between economic growth and exploitation, it's essential to acknowledge that these forces are not monolithic entities. Economic growth takes on various forms in different societies and contexts. It can be inclusive, benefiting a broad spectrum of the population, or exclusive, concentrating wealth and power in the hands of a few.

Similarly, exploitation is not a one-size-fits-all concept. It encompasses a wide range of injustices, from labor exploitation in sweatshops to environmental exploitation through reckless resource extraction. Recognizing these nuances is crucial in crafting solutions that strike a balance between progress and ethics.

Moreover, the dichotomy between economic growth and exploitation is not static. It evolves over time as societies mature and their values shift. What may have been considered acceptable in the pursuit of growth in the past may now be seen as morally unacceptable. This evolving perspective underscores the importance of ongoing dialogue and adaptation in our quest for a just and prosperous world.

In our pursuit of a harmonious coexistence between growth and justice, we must also recognize the role of leadership and governance. Governments, businesses, and civil society organizations play pivotal roles in shaping the trajectory of economic growth and mitigating exploitation. Effective policies, regulations, and corporate responsibility initiatives can make a significant difference in ensuring that growth benefits all members of society.

Education and awareness are equally crucial components of the solution. When individuals are informed about the consequences of unchecked growth and exploitation, they can advocate for change and make more responsible choices as consumers and citizens. Empowering people with knowledge is a potent tool in the quest for a fairer and more sustainable world.

The global community, too, has a role to play. In an increasingly interconnected world, addressing issues of economic growth and exploitation requires international cooperation. Global agreements on labor rights, environmental protection, and fair trade can set standards that transcend national boundaries and promote ethical practices on a global scale.

As we contemplate this perpetual struggle, it's important to remember that the tension between economic growth and exploitation is not a zero-sum game. It is possible to achieve both prosperity and justice, but it requires a deliberate and conscientious effort. By embracing a mindset that values ethical growth, sustainable practices, and social equity, we can steer the course toward a future where the benefits of progress are shared by all.

In conclusion, the interplay between economic growth and exploitation is a defining challenge of our time. It tests our collective wisdom, ethics, and capacity for change. While economic growth holds the promise of prosperity, it must be harnessed responsibly to avoid the pitfalls of exploitation. The path forward lies in our ability to strike a dynamic balance, adapt to evolving circumstances, and demand accountability from those who shape our world. In this ongoing dialogue, may we find the path that leads to a brighter, fairer, and more sustainable future for all.

CHAPTER FORTY-THREE

Innovation's Edge: Creativity versus Destruction

In the grand theater of societal evolution, there are two key players—Creativity and Destruction. These two forces, often intertwined and paradoxical, shape the narrative of human existence. They occupy center stage in the grand drama of human endeavors, captivating our attention with their contrasting acts that leave indelible marks on our world.

Creativity, adorned in a vibrant costume woven from threads of inspiration and ingenuity, takes our breath away with its brilliance. It is the muse that births art, science, and progress, crafting symphonies from silence, erecting architectural marvels that touch the sky, and penning stories that resonate through the ages. Creativity is the driving force behind innovation, continually pushing boundaries and challenging the status quo. It has the power to uplift our spirits, inspire our minds, and redefine our understanding of what is possible in the realms of human achievement.

Yet, even as Creativity dazzles with its virtuosity, lurking in the shadows is Destruction, a mysterious figure shrouded in darkness. Destruction's reputation is tainted by chaos, upheaval, and devastation. It wields the sword of recklessness, threatening to unravel the intricate tapestry of human progress. Destruction can emerge from misguided intentions, the relentless pursuit of progress at any cost, or the unforeseen consequences of creative endeavors gone awry.

Herein lies the paradox that defines the human condition—a precarious tightrope between Creativity and Destruction. Creativity, driven by noble intentions, can inadvertently pave the way for Destruction. Innovations conceived to enhance our lives may birth unforeseen consequences, from environmental catastrophes triggered by industrial progress to the misuse of advanced technologies with devastating consequences. The pursuit of artistic expression may inadvertently lead to the erasure of cultural heritage, and the relentless quest for progress can often leave marginalized communities in the shadows.

Conversely, Destruction, often cloaked in malevolent intent, can sometimes serve as an unintentional catalyst for rebirth and renewal. The crumbling of old orders can clear the path for new beginnings, sweeping away oppressive regimes and outdated ideologies. Catastrophes can inspire resilience, uniting communities in the face of adversity, and the ruins of the past can become the sturdy foundations upon which a brighter future is built.

Thus, we find ourselves entangled in this eternal tug of war, where the line that separates Creativity and Destruction is thin, and the consequences of each act reverberate through time. As stewards of this world, it is our solemn duty to harness the boundless energy of Creativity while remaining vigilant against the shadow cast by Destruction. We must tread this precarious path with wisdom, empathy, and a deep understanding that the true power of innovation lies not solely in its creation but in its far-reaching impact.

In the grand theater of human endeavors, let us aspire to orchestrate a harmonious duet where Creativity and Destruction dance not in discord but in tandem. May our pursuit of progress be tempered by a profound respect for the consequences of our actions. Let us endeavor to shape a world in which Creativity guides us towards a brighter future, and if Destruction must make an appearance, let it be solely as a catalyst for transformation and renewal. In this delicate balance, we may uncover the true potential of our shared human journey—a narrative enriched by the intertwined forces of creation and transformation, where our actions today echo through the annals of time, leaving an enduring legacy for generations yet to come.

To further contemplate the dynamic interplay between Creativity and Destruction, let us delve deeper into the realm of Creativity. It is the spark that ignites the fire of human innovation, the divine source of our most profound achievements. Creativity is the genesis of art, the muse that inspires poets to compose verses that resonate with the deepest recesses of our souls. It is the crucible of scientific discovery, driving minds to unlock the mysteries of the universe and harness the power of nature for the betterment of humanity.

Creativity knows no bounds, transcending the limits of time and space. It is the beacon that guides explorers to chart uncharted territories, the brush that paints strokes of beauty onto the canvas of existence, and the melody that soothes our weary hearts. It is the essence of our humanity, the source of our ability to dream and imagine worlds beyond our own.

However, even in its boundless brilliance, Creativity is not without its pitfalls. It can lead us down the rabbit hole of hubris, where unchecked ambition blinds us to the consequences of our actions. The pursuit of innovation can sometimes disregard ethical considerations, leaving us with the dilemma of whether we should do something simply because we can. Creativity's relentless quest for progress can sometimes overshadow the values of empathy and compassion, leading to a world that prizes achievement over the well-being of its inhabitants.

In contrast, Destruction emerges as a stark contrast to the brilliance of Creativity. It wears the cloak of chaos and upheaval, often serving as the antithesis to order and stability. Destruction can be swift and merciless, obliterating the creations of Creativity in its path. Yet, it is important to recognize that Destruction is not always the harbinger of doom. Sometimes, it is the harbinger of necessary change.

Destruction can arise from the shadows when the status quo becomes oppressive, when systems and structures crumble under the weight of their own flaws. It can serve as a wake-up call, urging us to reevaluate our priorities and reforge our path. In the wake of Destruction, there is often an opportunity for renewal and growth, a chance to build something stronger and more resilient from the ashes of the past.

In this complex dance between Creativity and Destruction, we must navigate the blurred lines with discernment and humility. We must recognize that both forces are integral to the human experience, intertwined in ways that challenge our understanding. Our task is not to choose one over the other but to find the delicate balance that allows them to coexist harmoniously.

As we contemplate the intricate interplay of Creativity and Destruction, let us be mindful of the responsibility that comes with our role as actors in this grand theater of life. Let us harness the power of Creativity to create a world of wonder and innovation, guided by wisdom and empathy. Let us acknowledge the potential of Destruction as a catalyst for necessary change, tempered by our commitment to rebuild with resilience and compassion.

Ultimately, the true measure of our humanity lies in our ability to navigate the eternal drama of Creativity and Destruction with grace and purpose, to recognize the profound impact of our actions, and to leave a legacy that illuminates the path for generations yet to come.

Author's Profile

Parth Ajit Khajgiwale is currently pursuing a Bachelor's degree in Computer Engineering at International Institute of Information Technology Pune. Apart from his academic endeavors, he has emerged as a prolific writer and a discerning blogger. Parth's journey in life is marked by an unquenchable thirst for knowledge and a relentless quest for self-discovery.

His initiation into the world of writing dates back to his 8th-grade years. Despite harboring a profound passion for the written word, he initially hesitated to share his creations. This hesitation stemmed from the illustrious contributions of his elder brother to the school magazine, which seemingly set a high benchmark. However, the advent of social media platforms such as Instagram and the world of blogging on Medium provided Parth with the much-needed confidence to express his thoughts and emotions.

He is recognized for his writing style, which deftly blends elements of expository and narrative approaches. His writing resonates deeply with readers, as it establishes an emotional connection and fosters meaningful engagement.

The primary source of inspiration for Parth is his family, especially his parents and elder brother. Their unwavering support and encouragement not only motivate him but also serve as a profound source of inspiration, driving his creative pursuits.

His motivation lies in his profound curiosity about the dualities that shape our existence. He draws parallels between life's dual facets and a coin with two faces—one celebrated, the other often overlooked. It is this innate curiosity that propels him to explore and articulate these dualities with creativity and insight.

His writing is aimed at readers who possess an introspective nature, an openness to explore complex themes, and a keen interest in unraveling the multifaceted aspects of life. His work is particularly appealing to those who seek a deeper understanding of the world and the intricate tapestry of the human experience.

One poignant personal experience that profoundly influenced his perspective and writing is witnessing the resilience and grace with which his parents navigated life's challenges. Their ability to find beauty even in adversity and their unwavering support for their children left an indelible mark on his outlook.

Instagram: *@versevirtuoso_*
Twitter:*@versevirtuoso_*
Email: parth.khajgiwale@gmail.com

Parth extends his heartfelt gratitude to his parents and elder brother for their unwavering support and inspiration throughout his writing journey. Their encouragement has been the driving force behind his creative endeavors. He also expresses sincere appreciation to his readers who have embraced his work, providing valuable feedback that fuels his creative process and inspires him to explore life's dualities with greater depth and conviction.

www.ingramcontent.com/pod-product-compliance
Lightning Source LLC
LaVergne TN
LVHW041208150826
845673LV00001B/324